The Birth of Churches

A Biblical Basis for Church Planting

The Birth
of
Churches

Talmadge R. Amberson
Compiler/Contributor

BROADMAN PRESS
Nashville, Tennessee

4263-17
ISBN: 0-8054-6317-8

Dewey Decimal Classification: 262
Subject heading: CHURCH

Library of Congress Catalog Card Number: 78-74149
Printed in the United States of America.

Preface

In the late spring of 1976 the Church Extension Department of the Home Mission Board of the Southern Baptist Convention brought together a group of church extension specialists from across the nation to share ideas and receive some additional training so that they could be used in conferences and consultation to undergird church planting. The Bold Mission Thrust was "on the pad for launch" with its emphasis on *evangelize* and *congregationalize*. The Home Mission Board was committed to sharing the gospel with every person in the nation so that each individual might have the opportunity to respond to Jesus Christ as Lord and Savior and be gathered together in responsible membership in a local church.

At this training session I was asked to lead the group in studies on the biblical basis for church planting. At that time and following the conference, several of the group requested that the material be expanded and made available to them in written form. Their requests stirred some interest and the possibility of a book of this nature was probed. The idea then cooled off and lay dormant for a while. Several months later it was again considered.

Jack Redford and I agreed that a book of this nature should be done by a group of writers. Therefore, a writing team was decided on, enlisted, and met for the first time in early 1977 in Atlanta. Before the meeting each of the team was given the synopsis of the original material which they were to read. The team discussed at length the material and possible subject matter for other chapters, keeping in mind that the book should center on the biblical material for church planting. Certain areas of ecclesiology, thereby, were eliminated.

The team had determined the subject matter which they felt needed to be covered and determined assignments. In the fall of 1977 the

team came back together as a group in a session along with the staff
of the Church Extension Department in which each man presented
the chapter he had written and the entire group joined in a critique
of his work. The writers then rewrote their material in light of this
dialogue.

The members of the team are well qualified in every way to write
a book of this nature. Eight of the men are native sons of the old
territory of the Southern Baptist Convention, while one is a native
of the newer areas. All have served churches as pastors and in other
positions of leadership. Two of the men have served as foreign missionaries for the Southern Baptist Convention; six in different capaci-
ties in the new areas of Southern Baptist work in the nation where
they have been related with the Home Mission Board; and one as
director of missions at two places in the South. Those who have
served in places of leadership across the new area have been involved
with churches, associations, or state conventions located in the geographical areas of the Northeast, North Central, Midwest and West.
In addition to serving as pastors, four have served as associational
directors of missions; one as associational director of church extension; one as a state director of church extension; one as both a state
director of Sunday School and state director of missions at different
times; one as editor of a state Baptist paper; two as foreign missionaries; three as seminary professors; one on the staff of the Home Mission
Board; and one as a full-time evangelist.

I wish to thank Jack Redford, director of the Church Extension
Department, for asking me to do the Bible studies out of which this
book grew and for his supervision, direction, counsel, and encouragement along the way in the process of the book. I also thank the
members of the writing team and compliment them on an assignment
well executed. I am grateful as well to the others on the staff of the
Church Extension Department in addition to Jack Redford and Quentin Lockwood—Nelson Tilton, David Benham, and William Slagle
for their part in the dialogue which helped in producing the book.
I, likewise, deeply thank the secretaries at the Home Mission Board,
as well as those who did work for various members of the writing
team, for their part in typing the manuscripts.

All biblical references quoted are from the *New American Standard*

Bible unless otherwise noted. When other versions are used the authors will give the particular one quoted for that specific citation.

Talmadge R. Amberson
Stone Mountain, Georgia

Contents

1
The Foundation for Church Planting

Talmadge R. Amberson

Does the Bible support the planting (the beginning) of churches? In the Bible is the establishment of new congregations/churches a part of God's redemption plan? Why do we need churches? Who make up the church? What in the life and ministry of Jesus supports the planting of churches? Did the Christians of the first century go out across the world and start new churches? Does the New Testament contain any elements which can be put together in a strategy for planting churches? Who is responsible for planting churches?

Talmadge R. Amberson is a full-time evangelist and Bible conference leader. A native of Alabama, he was graduated in 1952 with a Bachelor of Arts degree from Howard College (now Samford University). He received a Bachelor of Divinity degree in 1955 and a Doctor of Theology degree in 1961 from Southwestern Baptist Theological Seminary. He has done postdoctorate work at Wayne State University, Detroit, Michigan, and Fuller Theological Seminary.

He has served churches as pastor in Alabama, Texas, Missouri, Indiana, and Michigan; as director of associational missions in Detroit, and as a special consultant with the Home Mission Board of the Southern Baptist Convention. He has written a weekly article for the local newspaper in Scottsboro, Alabama, and has written various items for Southern Baptist publications.

The biblical foundation for the planting of churches has been assumed rather than explicitly set forth. Even the general concept of a theology of missions is almost overlooked or completely ignored.[1] Major works on systematic and biblical theology give very little emphasis to the biblical and/or theological foundation for missions, evangelism, church extension, and church planting. Some more recent writings set forth the biblical field with regard to missions and evangelism but information on the subject of church planting is almost totally lacking.

Works in the field of ecclesiology proper do acknowledge that the church should engage itself in witness, evangelism, proclamation, and missions. Though they use these and other terms which can be construed as inclusive of church planting, the writings on ecclesiology in most cases do not explore the entire scope of the beginning of new churches. They are almost totally silent concerning deliberate effort by which the Holy Spirit might bring into existence another visible structural entity—another local church—that is a part of the spiritual body of Christ.

The ultimate intent of this study is to undergird and motivate churches to plant new churches. The purpose is to encourage churches in sharing the gospel so that people can be discipled completely for Jesus Christ, both in a personal commitment to him as Lord and Savior as well as incorporation into a church in which the person can worship, fellowship, mature, witness, and minister.

The church is to begin at the place where it is located in its missions effort and, at the same time, reach out to all of the world. W. O. Carver wrote:

> Geographical distinction seems to lie at the base of the division in Acts 1:8. . . . Here is not quite our distinction between "home" and "foreign" missions, nor yet that of "city," "territorial" and "general." Not more than one of the Eleven was at home in Jerusalem. Rather they are to begin where they are and gradually to extend their scope until they come to the uttermost parts of the earth. The evangelized territory is not to be abandoned nor left whole to itself. That is clear enough. But when the cause is established in a centre, some are to move on thence to new territory.[2]

Baptists generally concede Carver's concepts to be the format for witnessing and missions. Do these assertions, which are an acceptable understanding of the mandate of the Great Commission (Matt. 28:19-20, and other parallel concepts in Mark 16:15; John 20:21; and Luke 24:46-49) also include and involve church planting?

The imperative to plant new churches is firmly grounded in the biblical revelation concerning God's interest in all mankind, as well as the procedure which God has used to communicate his message of love and salvation to men everywhere throughout the years. The foundation for church planting, as is true with all evangelism and mission endeavors, begins with the general missionary thrust of the Bible. It is then undergirded by the fact that those people who have responded to God's love through faith, thereby becoming rightly related to him, are used by God as instruments or vessels to communicate his message to others. Finally, the foundation was firmly and securely laid when, in the New Testament, churches clearly came into existence. Church planting simply took place as the believers of the first century witnessed of Jesus Christ and individually responded to accept him as Lord and Savior.

The Missionary Thrust of the Bible

The essence of biblical revelation concerning God's love and activity to redeem sinful man and the mission thrust of the Bible are exactly the same. God's love for sinful man is so great that he initiated and provided the act necessary for man's deliverance from sin (John 3:16; Rom. 5:8). Man is called to respond to God's love and be saved (Isa. 45:22; Matt. 11:28; John 7:37-39; Rom. 10:1-13; Eph. 2:4-8; Rev. 22:17).[3] God, having provided righteousness for individuals, now beseeches them through his ambassadors that they will receive the reconciliation which he has made possible (2 Cor. 5:18-21). As he calls men to respond, he uses men who have already responded through whom he extends the gospel to others. "How shall they hear without a preacher? And how shall they preach unless they are sent?" (Rom. 10:14-15). The missionary thrust of the Bible will be reviewed very briefly since it is so thoroughly known and affirmed.

God is creator and sustainer of the world and all within it (Gen. 1:1 to 2:25; Col. 1:16-17). Because he is Creator and Sustainer, God is also the rightful owner of all he has made (Ex. 19:5; Ps. 24:1; 50:12;). He also created man (Gen. 1:26-27; 2:7; Ps. 8:3-8; Acts 17:26).

God, the creator of man, shows throughout the Bible his interest in and intent for mankind. He tells Abram that in him "all the families of the earth shall be blessed" (Gen. 12:3). Later, he makes known his salvation and righteousness to all nations (Ps. 98:2-4). God's concern for all mankind is more prominent in the prophets (Isa. 2:4; 11:6-9; 45:22; 49:6; 52:10; Jer. 3:17; 16:19-21; Mic. 4:2-5; Hab. 2:14; 3:3; Zech. 2:11). His interest in all men was somewhat similar to a seed in his early revelation; the sprouting plant in the prophets; then bursting forth in full form in the New Testament (John 3:16). He has made all men (Acts 17:26) and now has provided abundant life for them through his Son, the Lord Jesus Christ (John 10:8-11). God sends the individuals who have come to salvation through Christ out into the world to make disciples of all nations (Matt. 28:19-20). The climax of God's interest in all men comes to completeness in John's vision on Patmos. "I looked and behold, a great multitude, which no man could count, from every nation and all tribes and people and tongues, standing before the throne and before the Lamb, clothed in white robes, and palm branches were in their hands; and they cry out with a loud voice, saying, 'Salvation to our God who sits on the throne, and to the lamb' " (Rev. 7:9-10).

Man, created by God and in the image of God (Gen. 1:26-27), is a sinner. Adam and Eve in the Garden of Eden disobeyed the command of God, took the fruit of the forbidden tree, and ate of it. As a result, God put them out of the Garden and the judgment for their sins came on them (Rom. 5:12-14). As in the case of Adam, all persons come to a point of decision and disobey God. Because he is a sinner, each individual is alienated from God and under the penalty of death (Ezek. 18:4; Rom. 1:18-24; 5:12-14; 6:21,23; 8:6-8; Jas. 1:15). While he may be living physically, the sinner separated from Christ and without God actually now is dead in his trespasses and sin (Eph. 2:1-3,5,12).

Although man is a sinner, God loves him (John 3:16) and sent his Son into the world to die, paying the penalty for man's sin (Rom. 5:6-9; 6:23). Jesus Christ, God's Son, went to the cross and there bore man's sin (1 Pet. 2:21-24). As the Lamb of God (John 1:29), he died for man's sin (1 Cor. 15:3-4) and gave his life as a ransom for many (Mark 10:45; Matt. 20:28). As High Priest, Jesus did not offer the blood of calves and goats but rather his own blood to cleanse sinful man (Heb. 9:11-14; cf. 2:9). He became the guarantee of a new covenant and is able to save forever those who draw near to God through him (Heb. 7:15-28). He delivers man from the curse of the law, the penalty of sin (Gal. 3:10-13), as he became accursed for the sinner. Jesus Christ frees sinful man from the body of death and the law of sin (Rom. 7:24-25).

In Christ's death God is at work reconciling the world to himself (2 Cor. 5:19). In Christ, man, who was separated from God, has been brought near to God, as all are gathered together in the "one new man" (Eph. 2:12-18). Thus man is reconciled to God and to his brother. Because we have redemption and the forgiveness of sin in Jesus Christ, God "has qualified us to share in the inheritance of the saints in light" (Col. 1:12) and has "delivered us from the domain of darkness and transferred us to the kingdom of His beloved Son" (Col. 1-13).

However, the sinner must repent of his sin and commit himself by faith to the Lord Jesus Christ if he is to experience the forgiveness of sin and the salvation available through Christ. Jesus in his earthly ministry asserted that he came to call sinners to repentance (Matt. 9:13; see the parallel passages in Mark 2:17 and Luke 5:32). He sent forth the twelve who "preached that men should repent" (Mark 6:12). Jesus also stated the necessity of repentance (Luke 13:3) and indicated the joy which abounded in heaven because one sinner repented (Luke 15:7). Peter in Acts indicated the significance of repentance (Acts 2:38; 3:19). Paul said, "God is now declaring to men that all everywhere should repent" (Acts 17:30). He also stated that the kindness of God leads men to repentance (Rom. 2:4). Paul wrote that "the sorrow that is according to the will of God produces a repentance without regret, leading to salvation" (2 Cor. 7:10). Peter affirmed that God is patient toward man, "not wishing for any to perish but for all to come to repentance" (2 Pet. 3:9).

In addition to repenting of his sin, the individual is to believe in Christ, that is, to trust or commit himself to the Lord Jesus Christ. To the one who does so Christ grants the power that he may become a son of God (John 1:12; see 3:16). Those who believe in Christ are also spoken of as being born of God (John 1:13; 3:3-8). To the direct question concerning what one must do to be saved, Paul answered, "Believe in the Lord Jesus, and you shall be saved" (Acts 16:31). Repeatedly, the writer of the Fourth Gospel emphasized the same truth as he indicated that by believing in Jesus Christ the individual possesses eternal life (John 3:18; 3:36; 5:24; 6:68-69; 7:37-39; 8:24). Paul asserted that the individual must believe in his heart that God has raised Jesus from the dead then with his mouth must confess Jesus as Lord (Rom. 10:8-13). He also declared that God by his grace or unmerited favor saves a sinful man when that man in faith turns to Jesus Christ (Eph. 2:8-9).

The one who has accepted Jesus Christ as Savior not only receives salvation but he is also brought into God's work and used as an instrument or vessel to share the gospel of Jesus Christ with others. The believer is incorporated by—baptized by—the Spirit of God into the body of Christ (1 Cor. 12:13). He is also the recipient of at least one gift from the Holy Spirit which enables him to build up the group of believers (1 Cor. 12:4-12). All persons who come to know Christ as personal Savior have, as a special act out of the grace of God through a gift or gifts of God's Spirit, been equipped to perform some service for the Lord's sake. As every member of man's physical body has a function to perform for the well-being as well as the growth of the physical body, so every member of the body of Christ—the church—has a function in the well-being and the growth of the church (1 Cor. 12:14-27). Jesus makes clear to us today, as he did to his disciples while he was here on earth, that we have not chosen him, but rather he has chosen us in order that we might bring forth fruit to the glory of God (John 15:16).

However, we who are chosen are not simply passive instruments in his hands, but rather must yield or commit ourselves constantly afresh unto him to be used for his work. In the context of the passage discussed above (John 15:1-17), Jesus stated that his followers are to abide in him (vv.4-7), prove their discipleship (v.8), and keep his commandments (vv. 10,12,17), possibly even to the point of sacrificing one's life (v.13). We as believers, recipients of God's gift of salvation, are "created in Christ Jesus for good works . . . that we should walk in them" (Eph. 2:10). We are to be a people for God's own possession, zealous for good deeds (Titus 2:14). In light of our anticipated resurrection, we are to be "abounding in the work of the Lord" (1 Cor. 15:58). Paul appeals to us even today that we present our bodies as living sacrifices to God which are worthy of being received by God and is our spiritual service of worship whereby we demonstrate to the world the good and perfect will of God (Rom. 12:1-2).

When God uses us in his work we become God's fellow workers in his field or building (1 Cor. 3:1-15; especially v.9). As bond servants of Jesus Christ, we become stewards of the mysteries of God (1 Cor. 4:1). We today are sent as the Father sent his Son into the world (John 20:21; see 17:18). As Jesus used the twelve (Matt. 10:1-23; Mark 6:7-13; Luke 9:1-6) or the seventy (Luke 10:1-16) during his ministry here on earth, he uses those at the present time who come to know him as Lord and Savior to carry the gospel to those who do not know him. We today who are his disciples are commissioned by him to make disciples for him (Matt. 28:19-20; Mark 16:15; Luke 24:46-49; John 20:21) and are to be his witnesses (Acts 1:8). God uses us to share the message of salvation with a world that does not know Christ.

The People of God

Church planting is essential because God is calling and using a people designated as his own. This he did in the Old Testament, when he called Abraham, and in the New Testament, when the people of his choice became the church. In Genesis 12:1-3, God spoke to Abram, promising to bless him and at the same time calling him to be a blessing to all of the nations of the earth. In Exodus 19, when God brought the descendants of Abraham out of bondage in Egypt, he called on them to obey his voice and keep his covenant [4] then they would be to him a people of his own possession among all of the people of the earth (v.5). God told Moses that the children of Israel were to be to him "a kingdom of priests and a holy nation" (v.6). When Moses gave God's message to the people, they "answered together and said, 'All that the Lord has spoken we will do!' " (v.8). Later the people said to Moses, " 'Go near and hear all that the Lord our God says; then speak to us all that the Lord our God will speak to you, and we will hear and do it.' " (Deut. 5:27). The people pledged themselves to hear God and do what God wanted them to do. God had made them his people and wanted to use them as they obeyed him to show other people that they were his people and thus through them the kind of God he was. The Palestinian Covenant (Deut. 30), a call to the people issued by God through Moses toward the end of his life, was a recommitment in Moab to the covenant which God had made with them at Horeb (Deut. 29:1). Moses called them to love God and obey his voice (Deut. 30:19-20).

The end to the Mosaic-Palestinian covenant as the Israelites understood it came during the ministry of Jesus. As he was teaching in the Temple the chief priests and the elders of the people asked him, "By what authority are You doing these things, and who gave You this authority?" (Matt. 21—23).

Jesus responded by asking the Jewish religious leaders by what authority John performed his baptism. When they refused to answer Jesus' question about John's authority, Jesus refused to respond to their challenge concerning his authority (Matt. 21:24-27). He then told the parable of the two sons (Matt. 21:28-32), indicating that the tax collectors and harlots who had heard John and responded to his message were doing the will of God. The chief priests and elders who did not respond to God's message through John were clearly implied to be the son who said he would do the father's will, then did not do it.

Jesus continued by telling the parable of the wicked tenant farmers (Matt. 21:33-39). Jesus then asked the Jewish leaders what the owner of the vineyard would do to these vine growers when he came. This judgment pronounced on the tenant farmers was actually a condemnation of themselves. Jesus, therefore said, "The Kingdom of God will be taken away from you, and be given to a nation producing the fruit of it" (Matt. 21:43).

When the Jewish religious leaders heard the words of Jesus, they understood.clearly that he was talking about them (see Matt. 21:45-46). They knew that the vine was a symbol of the nation (Ps. 80:8-9). They easily connected the words of Jesus in the parable of the wicked tenant farmers with the song of the beloved in the prophet Isaiah (Isa. 5:1-6) where the vineyard is identified as the nation of Israel (Isa. 5:7). "Here plainly is judgment on the old Israel." [5] Israel's mission had been to make known that God was the God of all men, but the nation had become self-centered. "Because, therefore, she abandoned her mission to the world, Israel was doomed." [6]

The inescapable conclusion is that the mantle designating the political nation of Israel as God's people was being passed to someone else. The Jewish people had confused the people of God with those people who were physically the descendants of Abraham. Two factors help us at this point to reassess the situation and determine the people of God. The first factor is an examination of the New Testament to find the same terminology and concepts used in God's dealings with his people in the Old Testament which are applied to the individuals who by faith have committed themselves to Jesus Christ. The second factor is to examine the idea of a "new covenant" and truths related to it both in the Old Testament and the New Testament.

Concepts Designating the People of God

Peter, the one whose apostleship was to the Jewish people and with whom God "effectually worked . . . in his apostleship" (Gal. 2:8), wrote some words in his first epistle (1 Pet. 2:4-9) which shed light on our study at this point. In referring to those who are Christian believers, Peter said that they "as living stones, are being built up as a spiritual house for a holy priesthood, to offer up spiritual sacrifices acceptable to God through Jesus Christ" (v.5). Then he identifies the believers as "a chosen race, a royal priesthood, a holy nation, a people for God's own possession" (v.9).

The words used by Peter here are similar to words in the Old Testament used to refer to Abraham and his descendants, although they are not in the immediate record of the initial calling of Abraham and God's acts in the lives of the other patriarchs. In addition, the words "choice," "choose," "elect," and "election" are not used to describe the encounter of God with the children of Israel under Moses at Sinai (Ex. 19:3-8; 24:2-7), but the other words of 1 Peter or words with similar ideas are there. However, the concept of God choosing them is present in the Exodus account and the specific words indicating God's choice or election are later used in the Bible to describe God's acts. Abraham, others of the patriarchs, the Hebrew slaves who were in bondage in Egypt, and their successors are referred to as:

(1) *A chosen or elect people, a people of God's choice* (The Hebrew word in each case is from the same Hebrew root form: Deut. 4:37-38; 7:6-8; 10:15; 14:2).

(2) *A priesthood or priest* (Ex. 19:6; Isa. 61:6. See Num. 3:6-13, where the Levites are chosen by God to minister for the entire congregation).

(3) *A holy nation or people, a consecrated people* (Ex. 19:6; Deut. 7:6; 14:2,21; 26:18-19; 28:9; Isa. 62:12; see Lev. 20:26; 21:6).

(4) *A people for God's own possession—literally "a special treasure"* (Ex. 19:5; Deut. 7:6; 14:2; 26:18; Mal. 3:17; see other words indicating the idea of ownership by or belonging to the Lord—Ex. 22:31; Lev. 20:26; Deut. 26:19; Ps. 33:12; 89:3; 135:4; Isa. 42:1; Jer. 33:24).

Peter's words (1 Pet. 2:9), or different words with parallel concepts, are used concerning Christian believers in other parts of the New

Testament. The twelve were chosen by Christ (Luke 6:13; John 6:70; 13:18; 15:16,19; Acts 1:2). Witnesses were chosen beforehand by God (Acts 10:41) to whom Christ became visible after his resurrection. Paul is noted as a "chosen instrument" (Acts 9:15). He also was a "bond-servant of God, and an apostle of Jesus Christ, for the faith of those chosen of God" (Titus 1:1) and was willing to "endure all things for the sake of those who are chosen" (2 Tim. 2:10). Rufus, "a choice man in the Lord," (Rom. 16:13) was one of the Christians in Rome. The members of a family or a church were chosen (2 John 1), and they, in turn, were greeted by the chosen members of a sister's family, or a sister church (2 John 13).

Believers in Christ are those who were chosen "before the foundation of the world" (Eph. 1:4), "from the beginning" (2 Thess. 2:13), "according to the foreknowledge of God the father (1 Pet. 1:1-2), and "chosen together" (1 Pet. 5:13) with other Christians. They are a part of the few who are chosen, although many are invited, to come to salvation (Matt. 22:14). They are chosen to fulfill the purpose of God (Rom. 9:11; 11:5,7,28:32). They know that God will "bring about justice for His elect" (Luke 18:7). They, as the elect, will have the days of tribulation cut short (Matt. 24:24; Mark 13:22) and will be gathered together to be with Christ when he comes again (Matt. 24:3; Mark 13:27). Believers in Christ, as God's elect, have no one who can bring a charge against them (Rom. 8:33). They are exhorted as the chosen of God to live the Christian life-style (Col. 3:12-17), thus indicating by the way in which they live their calling and choosing (2 Pet. 1:10, see vv. 2-11).[7] In the New Testament the Christian very definitely is a person chosen or elected by God, a person of election or a choice person.

In the second place, Peter called the Christians "a royal priesthood" (1 Pet. 2:9) and had written about them that "they as living stones, are being built up as a spiritual house for a royal priesthood" (1 Pet. 2:5). Elsewhere in the New Testament believers are referred to as priests or a priesthood in only two places. Christians are said to have been made by Christ to be "a kingdom, priests to His God and Father" (Rev. 1:6) and "a kingdom and priests to our God" (Rev. 5:10).

The tenet of the priesthood of every believer is basic to the New Testament. Jesus Christ is referred to as the mediator of "a new covenant" (Heb. 9:15; 12:24) and "a better covenant" (Heb. 8:6). He is the "one mediator also between God and men" (1 Tim. 2:5). The general movement in the ninth and tenth chapters of Hebrews is that the old sacrificial system has been done away with and now the believer has a new approach to God (Heb. 10:19-20). Every believer approaches God for himself and is not required to have a mediator other than Jesus Christ.

Every believer also as a part of the priesthood has the responsibility to come from the presence of God to make known God's will and way to man. The priest not only went into the presence of God for the people but he also came from God's presence back to the people for God.

Paul wrote of himself that the grace of God was given to him "to be a minister of Christ Jesus to the Gentiles, ministering as a priest the gospel of God" (Rom. 15:16). The phrase translated "ministering as a priest" in the Greek New Testament is one word—*hierourgeo*—which means to work as a priest and is related to the Greek words for *priest* and *priesthood.* The word "minister" in Romans 15:16 is the Greek word *leitourgos,* meaning a public worker or laborer. Another Greek word from the same root is *leitourgein* which is used to speak of service or ministry, both secular and religious (Luke 1:23; Acts 13:2; Rom. 13:6; 15:27; 2 Cor. 9:12; Phil. 2:17,25,30; Heb. 1:7, 14; 8:2,6; 9:21; 10:11). Paul was a minister performing his service or ministry as a priest unto God and his fellowman. This, the believer does.

The third term used by Peter, "a holy nation" (1 Pet. 2:9), does not occur at any other place in the New Testament. However, he wrote the words "a holy priesthood" (1 Pet. 2:5) in the immediate context. At other places in the New Testament, the same Greek word translated "holy" in the references in Peter is translated "saints" (plural) sixty-one times and "saint" (singular) one time. The *New American Standard Bible* translation for "saints" has a variant reading in the margin ("true believers; literally, *holy* ones") [8] at every place where it occurs. The significance of the plural, as well as the singular use (Phil. 4:21) where the adjective *every* is added, indicates a group or body of Christians. Saints are seen as more than one in number.

The word *saints* is from the Greek word *hagios* which means "set apart" or "separate." In addition to people, things or places may be holy so that the "fundamental idea is separation, and, so to speak, consecration and devotion to the service of Deity." [9] Thus, the idea of *hagios* is to separate or set apart some object, place, or person from everyday and common use to God's use, that is to dedicate that which is set apart to God's use. Therefore, when an individual commits himself in faith to Jesus Christ and accepts him as Savior, the forensic or positional aspect of sanctification is accomplished. Paul spoke of believers as "those who have been sanctified in Christ" (1 Cor. 1:2). W. T. Conner stated, "Every Christian, then, however imperfect he may be, is sanctified in the sense that he is dedicated or consecrated to God by the power of the Spirit and by his own act of faith." [10]

The believer becomes a part of a holy company of believers—the saints. While the forensic or positional aspect had no ethical or moral connotations, yet God's will for those who were his people in the Old Testament was that they would be like him (Lev. 11:44-45; 19:2; 20:7; see 1 Pet. 1:16). This longing on God's part confronts the saints or holy ones in the New Testament with the vital or dynamic aspect of sanctification. God wants to reproduce in his people those unique characteristics or qualities of God himself in order that they will be noted as his people. His people are to be holy as he is holy.

Finally, the last concept of Peter is found twice in the Pauline Epistles—"a people for his own possession" (Titus 2:14), and "of God's own possession" (Eph. 1:14). In Titus, Paul used a word for "possession" which is different from the one used by Peter. However, the thought of both men was influenced by the phrase in Malachi 3:17—"My own possession" ("special treasure," a variant reading—NASB, or "my jewels"—KJV). The words used by both Peter and Paul were used in the Septuagint translation of the Old Testament to express the same Hebrew terminology.[11] In addition, each of the men in his phraseology had the word *laos*. Richard C. Trench wrote "that *laos*, a word of rarest use in Attic prose, but occurring between one and two thousand times in the Septuagint, is almost always there a title reserved for the elect people, the Israel of God." [12]

In the Ephesian passage Paul did use the same word translated "possession" which is in 1 Peter 2:9, but he did not use the entire Petrinic phrase which included *laos*. In the use of the one word Paul has the equivalent of the Old Testament terminology "by which Israel is designated as the possession acquired by the Lord for himself (Ex 19:5; cf. Deut. 7:6; 14:2; 18; Ps. 135:4)." [13] In addition, this same Greek word translated "possession" (Eph. 1:14) occurs in three other places in the New Testament (1 Thess. 5:9; 2 Thess. 2:14; Heb. 10:39). These three uses of the word about that which the believer comes to acquire or possess—salvation, the glory of Christ, and the soul— add abundantly to the concept of "a people for God's own possession." God's people are those whom he acquires, gains, or comes to possess.

Peter, after his four affirmations concerning Christians (1 Pet. 2:9), used thoughts from the prophet Hosea. "You once were not a people, but now you are the people of God; you had not received mercy, but now you have received mercy" (1 Pet. 2:10; compare Hos. 1:6,9; 2:23). Paul also used the same words of Hosea (Rom. 9:25) and applied them to both Jewish and Gentile Christians (Rom. 9:24).

Peter and Paul both spoke of those who believed in Jesus Christ, Jew and Gentile alike, as those who had come to know the mercy of God and thus were called the people of God. To the affirmation of these two can also be added that of James, who at the Jerusalem conference stated that Peter "has related how God first concerned Himself about taking from among the Gentiles a people for His name" (Acts 15:14-15; see v. 17; Heb. 8:10). Peter had defended himself for his action at Cornelius' house by stating that God saved Cornelius and the others who heard and responded (Acts 11:15-18). God, by extending his mercy and saving them, had made them his own people or possession.

The next two Old Testament concepts which we examine are contained in each of the words *remnant* and *Israel*. These two concepts are found only in Pauline epistles. The significance of the use of *remnant* by Paul, however, cannot be found in a simple definition of the word. Its use in the Old Testament must be examined and its revelational, theological significance found to understand what is involved when Paul wrote about the remnant (Rom. 9:27; 11:5).

The word *remnant* meant simply the remainder, residue, or portion left, regardless of whether it referred to persons or things. In the Prophets, however, *remnant* designated a minority of the Israelites who would survive the destructive, refining, purging judgments brought upon them by God (Amos 9:8-12; Micah 2:12; 2 Kings 19:29-

31; 21:14; 2 Chron. 30:6; Isa. 1:9; 10:22; 37:31-32; Ezek. 11:13-21; 14:21-22; 23:25).

While a residue of survivors returned to rebuild the city of Jerusalem, the concept comes through that all which had been spoken concerning the remnant had not been accomplished. Ezekiel's prayer (Ezek. 11:13) before the fall of Jerusalem and Ezra's prayer after the rebuilding of the city (Ezra 9:14) have words which indicate the certainty that a remnant, a righteous remnant, must be in God's plan. The restoration of the remnant after the exile does not adequately fulfill the words of God given in answer to Ezekiel's prayer (Ezek. 11:15-20, especially vv 19-20).

Interwoven with the literal return of the group to Zion are ideas which are both messianic and eschatological so that the fulfillment of these cannot be accomplished short of the first and second advent of Christ. Some messianic concepts (Amos 9:11—"the fallen booth of David"; Isaiah 11:1—"the stem of Jesse, and a branch from his root"; Micah 5:2—"One will go forth for Me to be ruler in Israel") associate the thought with the first advent of Christ. However, the words of Micah concerning "the last days," "many nations" going "up to the mountain of the Lord," hammering "swords into plowshares And their spears into pruning hooks" and each man sitting "under his vine, and . . . fig tree" (Mic. 4:1-4) indicate a time that is eschatological, a time that has not yet arrived. In the fabric of thought woven by these varied concepts, people from other nations are included along with the remnant of Israel.

Paul wrote to the Christians at Rome, "There has also come to be at the present time a remnant according to God's gracious choice" (Rom. 11:5). Earlier he stated concerning God's choices that "He has mercy on whom He desires, and He hardens whom He desires" (Rom. 9:18).

God can do as he wills to demonstrate his wrath and make known his power. He has called, therefore, people from among both the Jews and Gentiles into his grace. While Paul expressed his heartbrokenness for his own brothers of the flesh, (Rom. 11:1; see 9:1-3), he left the door open to them at the same time (Rom. 11:23). God has a remnant. All who through God's gracious choice, his election, come to believe in Jesus Christ, his Son, become simultaneously a part of the remnant as well as the church, or body of Christ (Rom. 9:30-33).

A remnant has come to be at the present time as Jew and Gentile alike responded to the gospel. Some of the branches have been broken out of the olive tree which is a symbol of those who belong to God, and branches from the wild olive tree, Gentiles, have been grafted in among the branches left to become partakers of the rich root of the cultivated olive tree. Those thus brought by grace into the remnant are to be mindful that their status is because of the kindness and mercy of God (Rom. 11:17-22).

J. Robert Nelson, stated:

> Although Israel failed to obtain what it sought, the remnant of the elect, those chosen and summoned by God to know Jesus Christ had attained it [Romans 11:7]. It is plain to see how very adaptable the remnant idea was for Paul's explanation of the church, not merely as an analogy, however, but as a veritable identification of the Church with the Remnant which the prophets had described and foretold.[14]

The application of the name Israel to those who believe in the Lord Jesus Christ is the second uniquely Pauline concept witnessing to the continuity of the people of God in the Bible. The term *new Israel* which has been used to speak of the church, does not occur anywhere in Scripture, although the idea which it expresses is present. Paul used the term "the Israel of God" (Gal. 6:16) as a clear designation for the church. In Galatians, he had previously developed the thought "that it is those who are of faith that are the sons of Abraham" (Gal. 3:7). He concluded, "If you belong to Christ, then you are Abraham's offspring, heirs according to promise" (Gal. 3:29). To identify the body of believers as "the Israel of God," after his ethical exhortations, is in keeping with his theological foundation established earlier. Faith in Jesus Christ is the important thing. "For neither is circumcision anything, nor uncircumcision, but a new creation" (Gal. 6:15). God has brought all men into Christ and thereby created "the one new man" (Eph. 2:13-16). This is the true Israel of God, new men created in Christ Jesus when by the grace of God they are saved through faith (Eph. 2:8).

A concept from Matthew's Gospel converges with Paul's thought at this point. Matthew stated that the return of Mary and Joseph from Egypt with the young child Jesus, after the death of Herod, was in order that the word spoken by the prophet might be fulfilled (Matt. 2:15; see Hos. 11:1*b*). By implication, the name "Israel" is therefore applied to Jesus, since God's words to the prophet Hosea were clearly about the Egyptian bondage of the descendants of Jacob. At Peniel Jacob's name had been changed, after his encounter with God, to Israel (Gen. 32:24-31, especially v. 28). The descendants of the sons of Israel (Jacob) became the nation Israel. The significance of Matthew's words are that Jesus is the fountainhead of the people of God in the New Testament, the source of the Israel of God, the new Israel.

Another line of thought is also relevant at this place. In Romans Paul discussed "the children of promise" (Rom. 9:6-33). All who have descended physically from Israel are not Israel. Isaac was the son of promise and when Rebecca bore of him two sons, God chose Jacob. Paul declared that God's choice was not injustice on God's part, but rather his prerogative because of his divine sovereignty. The Israel of God is made up of those of promise, those whom God has chosen and called, both from among the Jews and Gentiles, who responded through faith to appropriate the righteousness of God (Rom. 9:23-33; 10:8-13; see Eph. 1:3-6; 2 Pet. 1:1-2). While Christ is the righteousness of God (Rom. 3:21-26), the source of the new Israel, man appropriates the righteousness, becomes a part of the Israel of promise by faith (Rom. 9:33). Those who are the people of faith are the sons of Abraham (Gal. 3:7).

Karl Barth stated: "This people of Jesus Christ is the people of God . . . . The people of God were never identical with the Jewish people as a national entity." [15] Israelites are not excluded, but rather the church, by virtue of the universal extent of its mission given by Jesus, "is the eschatological Israel, the Israel which receives into its life and history the chosen ones from among the Gentiles." [16] It can also be seen "as the Israel of the end time, fulfilling the destiny of the historical Israel, as 'a covenant to the people, a light to the nations' (Isa. 42:6, 49:8)." [17] The Christians of the New Testament era "knew themselves to be the heirs of all the ages and especially of the covenants made with the Jews. The church was the sphere of fulfillment of Israel's hope." [18]

The New Covenant

While the examination of these concepts establishes the continuity of the people of God throughout the entire Bible, the crux of determining who is numbered among the people of God from the time of the earthly ministry of Jesus Christ onward in history is the *New Covenant.* Isaiah, Jeremiah, and Ezekiel spoke of an "everlasting covenant" (Isa. 55:3; 61:8; Jer. 32:40; 50:5, Ezek. 37:26; see Gen. 17:7,13,19; 2 Sam. 23:5; Ps. 105:10). While the words "everlasting covenant" had been previously recorded in the Bible, the prophets spoke in contexts which all seem to require a different or new covenant. Other passages also point to this covenant which is anticipated (Isa. 54:13; 59:20-21; Jer. 24:7; Ezek. 11:19,20; 18:31; 36:26-28; 39:29; see 44:9).

While Ezekiel's words had significant concepts in them, Jeremiah was the first to speak clearly and specifically of a new covenant (Jer. 31:31-34). He stated that God said he would make a new covenant with Israel and Judah, which was different from the one he had made with their fathers. He also said that God would put his law in the hearts of the people; he would be their God, and they would be his people.

At the keeping of the Passover feast with his disciples, Jesus instituted the Lord's Supper. Against the background of the deliverance of the descendants of Jacob from bondage in Egypt (Ex. 12:41-50; 13:10; 34:18; Deut. 16:1-8, et. al.), Jesus established an observance to commemorate a more meaningful deliverance—the deliverance of those who would believe in him from the servitude of sin. On that night he said about the bread, "This is my body which is for you" (1 Cor. 11:24; see Matt. 26:26; Mark 14:22; Luke 22:19). And about the cup, "This cup is the new covenant in my blood" (1 Cor. 11:25; Luke 22:20; see Matt. 26:28, Mark 14:24, where the word "new" does not occur, only "My blood of the covenant").

The writer of the book of Hebrews spoke of a "new covenant" (Heb. 8:8-13; 9:15; 12:24) and a "better covenant" (Heb. 7:22; 8:6). He indicates that this new and better covenant is accomplished in and through the death of Jesus Christ. Paul wrote of a "new covenant," which is not of the letter but of the Spirit (2 Cor. 3:6).

The final outcome is that, through the death of Jesus Christ, God made it possible for the one who believes in Jesus to have forgiveness of sin and come into a new relationship with him in an eternal covenant (Heb. 13:20). In the "new" and "better" covenant, the law and will of God are written upon the hearts of men (compare Heb. 8:10; 10:16; 2 Cor. 3:6 with John 14:26; 16:13; Gal. 5:16,18). The entire movement of the letter to the Hebrews is that this new and better covenant exceeds, in the sense of fulfilling, any prior covenant between God and man (see Heb. 9:1 to 10:20).

How does this new covenant become operative in the life of an individual? How does one become a part of the people of God? When one takes Christ, that is, believes on him, he is granted by God the power to become a son of God (John 1:12). Through faith in Jesus Christ, one becomes a son of God (Gal. 3:26).

The transition from the word "people" to "sons" should not go unnoticed. God, out of his love (John 3:16; Rom. 5:8), sent his Son, who was called Jesus, into the world so that Jesus might save his people from their sins (Matt. 1:21). Christ Jesus gave himself for sinners that he might redeem them and purify for himself a people to be his own (Titus 2:14). During his earthly ministry Jesus, with the use of the term *Father,* brought a new intimate, personal concept of God (Luke 23:34,46; John 3:16; 5:17; 10:15; 14:2 et. al.) which had been present in the Old Testament, but undeveloped.

Paul, from Hosea, brought together the synonymous concepts, "people of God," and "sons of God." "And it shall be that in the place where it was said to them, 'You are not My people,' there they shall be called sons of the living God" (Rom. 9:26, where Paul quoted Hos. 1:10; see 2 Cor. 6:16-18, especially v. 18 where Paul used the words "sons and daughters" which reflect the idea of Isa. 43:6). One becomes through faith in Jesus Christ a part of the people of God, one of the children of God, a son, an heir, fellow heir with Christ (Rom. 8:14-17; 1 John 3:1; Gal. 4:7).

God's intention for man was not and is not now outward conformity through religious ceremonies, rituals, and institutions, but rather that man would bind himself to God in a faith relationship in which he loved God as well as desired to do God's will. As "Abraham believed God and it was reckoned unto him as righteousness . . . those who are of faith that are sons of Abraham" (Gal. 3:6-7). Paul's argument here is related to the new covenant in that God did not make his promise to Abraham and his seeds, but rather to Abraham and his

29

seed. The apostle asserted that the seed is Christ. The blessing of Abraham had thus come to the Gentiles in Christ Jesus as he died to remove all who were under the curse of death (Gal. 3:10-16).

Moses emphasized the desire of God to circumcise the heart of the Israelite so that he might love God (Deut. 30:6). Jeremiah exhorted the people of his day concerning a circumcision of a spiritual nature (Jer. 4:4). Neither circumcision nor uncircumcision is anything but rather keeping the commandments of God (1 Cor. 7:19), faith working through love (Gal. 5:6), a new creation (Gal. 6:15), or a renewal in which Christ is all and in all (Col. 3:11). Circumcision is a matter of the heart (Rom. 2:27-29), so that there is neither Jew nor Greek, slave nor free, male nor female, but rather all are one in Christ Jesus (Gal. 3:28). The people of the circumcision and those of the uncircumcision have been brought together in Christ, as the walls of separation have been broken down; and the enmity between the Jew and Gentile is put to death as the two are made one man in Christ (Eph. 2:11-22). All men have access in the one Spirit to the Father and are built together into a dwelling for the Spirit of God.

The Purpose of God's People

The final words about God's people are that God chooses and uses a people as his own so that others through them might come to know him and be a part of his people. Peter, after identifying God's own people, also made a statement about their purpose. "You are a chosen race, a royal priesthood, a holy nation, a people for God's own possession, that you may proclaim the excellencies of Him who has called you out of darkness into His marvelous light" (1 Pet. 2:9). The Greek word translated "excellencies" means "courage," "virtue," "force or strength of mind or body."

The people of God are to show or proclaim the excellencies, virtue, strength of God who has delivered them from sin and death into life. Paul, before King Agrippa, said that the Lord Jesus spoke to him,

> "For this purpose I have appeared to you, to appoint you a minister and a witness not only to those things which you have seen, but also to the things in which I will appear to you; delivering you from the Jewish people and from the Gentiles to whom I am sending you, to open their eyes so that they may turn from darkness to light and from

the dominion of Satan to God, in order that they may receive forgiveness
of sins and an inheritance among those who have been sanctified by
faith in Me" (Acts 26:16-18).

God's purpose for all of his people is to use them to open the eyes
of others and turn them to himself in order that he might save them.
Paul, speaking to the Jewish people at Rome, indicated the universal
scope of God's purpose, "Let it be known to you therefore, that
this salvation of God has been sent to the Gentiles; they will also
listen" (Acts 28:28). At Damascus God had instructed Ananias concerning Paul, "Go, for he is a chosen instrument of Mine, to bear
My name before the Gentiles and kings and the sons of Israel" (Acts
9:15). At Antioch in Pisidia, when the Jews began to contradict the
teaching of Paul, "Paul and Barnabas spoke out boldly and said, 'It
was necessary that the word of God should be spoken to you first;
since you repudiate it, and judge yourself unworthy of eternal life,
behold, we are turning to the Gentiles' "(Acts 13:46). Clearly, the
words of Paul to the Athenians are more true today than even when
spoken, "God is now declaring to men that all everywhere should
repent" (Acts 17:30).

The people of God having responded to the revelation of God
not only enter into a right relationship with him but also come to
understand God's purpose for man and have a responsibility to be
used to share that purpose, that mystery of God. They know that
through Christ Jesus all men, Jew and Gentile alike, are together
heirs of God, members of the body of Christ, the church, and recipients of God's promise. They also know that this revelation of God's
purpose is to be made known through the church (see Eph. 3:1-10).
They are aware that men who are separated from Christ are "excluded
from the commonwealth of Israel, and strangers to the covenants
of promise, having no hope and without God in the world" (Eph.
2:12). They have experienced the fact that, although they were in
this plight, the walls of enmity which divide men have been broken
down in Christ who made "one new man" as he reconciled all men
to God in himself on the cross (Eph. 2:13-16; see Gal. 3:28; Col.
3:10-11).

While all the Gospels give the mandate of mission and witness
from the lips of Jesus, no one of them does it more comprehensively

and dramatically, yet simply, than the Johannine words. Jesus held himself up then and holds himself up today as the model for the believer concerning the purpose the believer is to fulfill when he said, "As the Father has sent Me, I also send you" (John 20:21; see 17:18). The believer can look at the ministry of Jesus to see clearly the specifics which he should be doing to fulfill God's purpose for himself. "To be a member of Christ's body is to be involved with Him in all His concerns . . . . To belong to Him means to identify ourselves with all with whom He has identified Himself." [19]

Jesus was sent into the world because of God's love (John 3:16; 1 John 4:9-10) as well as to demonstrate that love (Rom. 5:6-8; Eph. 2:4-7). He, at the same time, showed his Father to men (John 14:8-11). He came not to be served but to serve (Matt. 20:28; Mark 10:45). "He went about doing good, and healing all who were oppressed by the devil" (Acts 10:38). Jesus taught (Matt. 4:23; 9:35; John 6:59; 18:20). He "proclaimed the gospel of the kingdom" (Matt. 4:23; 9:35; see Mark 1:14 and Luke 4:43, "the gospel of God"). He healed people of their afflictions and diseases (Matt. 4:23; 8:16; 9:35; 14:14; 15:30; 19:2; 21:14).

Jesus came, however, primarily "to seek and to save the lost" (Luke 19:10), "to give his life a ransom for many" (Mark 10:45; John 1:29). Jesus knew that he had come down among men to do the will (John 6:38; 5:30; 4:34; Luke 22:42) and work (John 4:36; 9:4; 17:4; see 19:28-30; 5:17-19) of God. He knew that God's work was for men to believe in him whom God had sent (John 6:28-29). He knew that God's will was that Christ would lose none of those who came to him, but rather raise them up in the resurrection because God's will was that every one who beheld and believed in the Son would have eternal life (John 6:38-40).

The people of God, the Christians, can and must do everything that Jesus Christ did except give his life as a ransom since Christ's death for man's sin is unique, sufficient, and not repeatable (Heb. 9:11-28). The people of God should be so controlled by the love of Christ (2 Cor. 5:14) as they are sent into the world that they do what Christ did. They should demonstrate God's love and show God himself to people. They are not to be served or ministered to, but rather to serve. They should "touch" people where they hurt, minister to them in their afflictions, illnesses, and problems of all nature. The people of God should teach, preach, proclaim, and witness about the good news of Jesus Christ—the gospel. They should do the will and work of God. They must do all that Jesus did except the one fact of providing salvation for men. However, "We [the people of God] know love by this, that He laid down his life for us; and we ought to lay down our lives for our brethren" (1 John 3:16). The statement is exceedingly strong because the principle of sacrifice is there for every child of God. Is not the believer under the obligation to even lay down his life if such an act is necessary in order that men may come to know Christ? This, in the will of God, is the ultimate purpose for the people of God in order that men may experience salvation (Rom. 12:1-2).

The responsibility of proclaiming the excellencies of God requires and produces intensive growth as well as extensive growth. Orlando E. Costas wrote, "Church growth is that holistic expansion which can be expected spontaneously from the everyday action of the church functioning as a redemptive community." [20] For him, "Church growth to be holistic expansion . . . must encompass four major areas: numerical, organic, conceptual, and incarnational." [21]

Intensive and *extensive,* words used here to delineate church growth, are chosen to attempt to make distinctions similar to Costas'. *Intensive growth* is that growth whereby the body of Christ through thorough, profound, exhaustive, concentrated efforts of worship, teaching, training, and other involvement in nurture more completely develops both its understanding of the nature and mission of the church and its organizational structure and activities so that the outreach, ministry, and life-style of its people in the world might be more effective. *Extensive growth* is that growth whereby the influence or scope of the church is expanded or extended so that the verbal witness, teaching, ministry, and life-style of its people not only impact the world at large with Christian teaching, concepts, thoughts and ethics but also confront individuals who are not Christian to respond in repentance from sin and faith in Jesus Christ and be brought into the fellowship of believers so that they, as new believers, become involved in the mission of the church.

These two types of growths are not independently exclusive but rather are mutually dependent. Either one without the other can produce a spiritual malignancy for the body of Christ. Both types of growth are dynamically and vitally related in the holistic concept. They must be interwoven and employed to produce not only numbers for the church in increased membership and an increase in the number of local churches but also to produce the kind of people who are the church—to produce believers and then, their continued growth as individuals into the "fulness of Christ" (Eph. 4:13; see 3:14-19).

If intensive growth, to use Costas' terminology,[22] is in the areas of growth identified as organic and conceptual expansion then a part of it is incarnational growth. Extensive growth is that which is identified as numerical expansion. A part of it is incarnational growth, yet to a greater degree than Costas seems to view the matter. Incarnational growth should impact people in general but it also should, by its very nature, confront men in such a fashion that they will respond to, want to know about, and accept Jesus Christ as Savior and Lord (see Acts 16:25-35). Incarnational growth should touch people not only at the point of their physical, emotional, and social needs but also at the point of their spiritual needs.

The people of God, the followers of Christ, are to expect intensive growth (Eph. 4:11-16) and the Jerusalem church did so (Acts 2:42-47). They are to anticipate extensive growth (Eph. 4:11-16) and the Jerusalem church did so (Acts 2:47; 4:4; 5:14; 6:7; 9:31,35,42; 11:21,24; 14:1,21; 16:5; 17:12). The Ephesian passage is of such nature that its truths are applicable to the specific local body of Christ (the local church) as well as the total spiritual body of Christ (all local churches). The extensive growth, as totally expressed here, cannot be accomplished without the planting of churches.

In addition, the purpose of proclaiming the excellencies of God has several factors which are absolutely essential if both intensive and extensive growth is to be realized. The people of God must be:

1. A people who worship God (Acts 1:14; 2:42-47; 5:42; 6:4; 20:7; Rom. 12:12; Col. 4:2).

2. A people who have a sense of fellowship and sharing (Acts 1:14; 2:42-47; 1 Cor. 10:16; 1 John 1:3,7).

3. A people who are growing or maturing in the Lord (Matt. 28:20; Acts 6:4; 1 Cor. 14:20; Eph. 4:11-16; Col. 1:28; see the call to move on from food for babies, 1 Cor. 3:1-3; Heb. 5:12-13; 1 Pet. 2:2-3

and God's intention for the Christian to be like Christ, Rom. 8:28-29; Phil. 3:14-21; Col. 3:9-11).

4. A people who witness to and proclaim the Lord Jesus Christ (Luke 24:48; John 15:27; Acts 2:6-8; 4:33; 10:34-42; 11:19-21; Rom. 10:13-15).

5. A people who minister in every way to show God's love, concern, and plan for men everywhere (John 20:21; Acts 10:38; Jas. 2:15-16, note that the context is a person without food or clothing; 1 John 3:16).

For the people of God to do these things as they ought to be done, a corporate body—a church—is necessary. The declaration of the excellencies or virtues of God as it produces Christians, that is, people who respond in faith to Jesus Christ, must emphasize too the necessity of the body of believers. The totality of sharing involves the incorporating of those who respond to the gospel into local churches. This inevitably results in the planting of churches which in turn follow the cycle through a similar process to produce other Christians and other churches.

God calls out a people who by faith in Jesus Christ become his people and uses them to confront other people with the message of Christ as they worship, fellowship, mature, witness, proclaim, and minister as a body—both the total body and also the local body—an assembled group of people at a particular point in time and place in space. For this to be accomplished requires churches—and church planting.

The Witness of the New Testament

In the final section we look at what actually happened in the New Testament that lends support to the planting of churches. We will notice in the Scriptures how the missionary thrust of the Bible and God's choice of people whom he used to share his blessings with others were woven together in the starting of new churches. We do not find a plan that is laid out and then unfolded, but rather we must follow the unfolding by examining that which occurs in the New Testament. We will begin with the ministry of Jesus himself and look at the work of the twelve he chose, then, finally the apostle Paul, other leaders, and churches of the New Testament era to see church planting develop.

The Life and Teaching of Jesus

Incidents related to three different persons at the time of the birth of Jesus bear witness to the continuity of God's people in the Old Testament. Before his birth God appeared to Zacharias to inform him that his wife, Elizabeth, would bear a son who was to be named John and was to be the forerunner of the Messiah as promised by Malachi (Luke 1:5-25; see Mal. 3:1; 4:5-6). Also, Simeon, (Luke 2:25-35), led to the Temple by the Holy Spirit when the parents of Jesus brought him there after his birth, took Jesus in his arms, blessed God, then prayed that God would now let him depart in peace. Likewise, Anna (Luke 2:36-38), who at the same time came up, began giving thanks to God and continued to speak of Jesus to all who were looking for the redemption of Jerusalem promised by the prophet (Isa. 52:9-10; see 42:6; 49:6) not only for Israel but also for the Gentiles.

The call of Jesus in his public ministry was given to individuals who responded to it personally and individually, thereby producing a group designated as *disciples* who made the embryonic church which was added to on the day of Pentecost (Acts 2:41). In response to his call, "follow me" (Matt. 4:18-25; 8:22; 9:9), these men who gathered about Jesus here on earth as his followers, genuinely and sincerely committed to him, constituted the church—his people.

Although one, who is identified as a devil (John 6:70-71) and the son of perdition (John 17:12), did not commit himself to Jesus, the others, however, at least by the time of the confession at Caesarea Philippi, did believe in him. Peter's confession, "Thou are the Christ, the Son of the living God" (Matt. 16:16), is the consensus of opinion for the entire group. These few words are the heart of the first statement of faith on the part of Christians (Matt. 10:32; Luke 12:8; John 6:68-69; Rom. 10:9-10,13). To believe in Christ is also to belong to him (John 17:6-10), as well as to belong to or be a part of his church (1 Cor. 10:16-17; Rom. 12:5; Eph. 2:14-16; 4:4).

The naming of twelve disciples by Jesus (Mark 3:14; Luke 6:13), where the number so obviously corresponds to the number of the tribes of Israel and the selection of a successor to Judas by the believers (Acts 1:15-26) definitely suggest a relationship with God's people of the Old Testament.

The twelve apostles were probably the nucleus to the new Israel. This is not mere speculation, for the idea of new Israel is itself secure in the New Testament, and the coupling of the twelve with new Israel is suggested.[23]

At the instituting of the Lord's Supper, while observing the Passover with his disciples (Matt. 26:17-30; Mark 14:12-26; Luke 22:7-30; John 13:1-38; 1 Cor. 11:17-29), Jesus stated, "Just as My father has granted Me a kingdom, I grant you that you may eat and drink at My table in My kingdom, and you will sit on thrones judging the twelve tribes of Israel" (Luke 22:29-30). John saw the new Jerusalem with twelve foundations on which are to be written the names of the twelve apostles (Rev. 21:14).

Other words, statements, and concepts used by Jesus give support to the same truth suggested by the naming of the twelve disciples. The first to note is a group of words—shepherd, flock, sheep, fold or pasture, which in a tremendously descriptive way pictures the relationship between God and his people as well as his protection and provision for them. Using the pastoral background of the Israelites, the Old Testament spoke of God as a shepherd (Ps. 23:1; Jer.31:10), his people as his flock (Ps. 77:20; 80:1; Isa. 63:11), his people as his sheep (Ps. 78:52; Ezek. 34:10-12), and God's restoration, care, or ownership as a fold or pasture for his sheep (Jer. 23:3; Ps. 23:2).[24]

Words which have the same background and connotations are used in the New Testament. Jesus spoke of himself as the "shepherd" (John 10:11,14) and with other words (John 10:1-23) also identified himself as the same. After indicating that the sheep were his because he was the good shepherd (John 10:11-15), he called them "my sheep" (John 10:27-28). He stated that he had "other sheep which are not of this fold" but that he would bring them as they heard his voice into "one flock with one Shepherd" (John 10:16). He addressed his disciples as a "little flock" (Luke 12:32) and announced to them that "the sheep of the flock shall be scattered" (Matt. 26:31). Jesus instructed Peter, "Tend My lambs" (John 21:15), "Shepherd My sheep" (John 21:16), "Tend My sheep" (John 21:17).

Paul, Peter, and the writer of Hebrews indicated that they understood that "flock" and "church" are words applied to the same people. Paul, exhorting the elders of the Ephesian church, used the noun "flock" and the verb "to shepherd" (Acts 20:28). Peter, as he challenged the elders to whom he wrote, used the word "shepherd" and twice penned the word "flock" (1 Pet. 5:2-3). The writer of Hebrews identified the God of peace as "the great Shepherd of the sheep" (Heb. 13:20).[25]

Jesus used another thought immediately after observing the Passover and instituting the Lord's Supper commemorating the new covenant. He said, "I am the true vine" (John 15:1), which identified him with the house of Israel as the vineyard of the Lord (Isa. 5:7).

> The depiction of the people of Israel in the Old Testament times as "a vine" was a figure of the true. "The true vine" is Christ. The new and true Israel is constituted in him. The true Israelites are not the Jewish Israelites . . . , who claim to be physically descended from Abraham, but the Christo-Israelites, whose one ground of belonging to Israel is that they belong to Christ.[26]

Twice Jesus used truths about human families to indicate truths about the relationship of believers to himself. He called people into a relationship through faith that could be compared to family ties (Matt. 12:46-50; Mark 3:33-35; Luke 8:19-21). He also indicated the way, "Whoever shall do the will of My Father" (Matt. 12:50; cf. Mark 3:35) and "these who hear the word of God and do it" (Luke 8:21), by which the spiritual family ties were established. In the context of words about discipleship, Jesus placed a deeper demand and expectation on a person than the demands which exist within one's own family (Matt. 10:37). "The idea of the people of God [the church] as a new family is inescapable." [27]

The *family of God* is a scriptural term related to Christians to express depths of meaning in the mutual relationship which exists between the believer and God, as well as the believer and other believers. The Holy Spirit, who is in the people who belong to Christ (Rom. 8:1-9), witnesses to the believers that they "are children of God" (Rom. 8:16) and "heirs also, heirs of God and fellow-heirs with Christ" (Rom. 8:17).

"Son of man is Jesus' favorite term for himself." [28] He used the term on numerous occasions, but beyond the Gospels the term rarely occurs. Stephen spoke of the "Son of Man" (Acts 7:56) and the book of Revelation twice has, "one like a son of man" (Rev. 1:13; 14:14), which W. T. Conner said is "evidently a reflection of Daniel 7:13." [29]

"Son of Man" is clearly used in the Old Testament to designate a man, a personality (Ps. 8:4; 144:3; Job 25:6). When it occurs more than ninety times in Ezekiel it describes the prophet as a frail human creature in the sight of almighty God.[30] In addition to the concept of man as a frail, weak being, a second idea is also in the Old Testament (Dan. 7:13-14) and had been, in the main, overlooked.

Jesus took the thoughts about the Son of man and the Suffering Servant (Isa. 42:1-4; 50:4-11; 52:13 to 53:12) and blended them together to enlighten the people about his role as Messiah. "He reinterpreted the idea of the Son of Man in terms of the Suffering Servant, not the Servant-conception in terms of the Son of Man."[31] In the light of Isaiah 53, as Jesus saw himself, "the Son of Man . . . is a new figure clothed with the marred form of the Servant."[32]

While the term *Son of Man* "truly designates Jesus as human and as the representative of humanity,"[33] it also has significance for the community of believers. The interpretation of the vision of Daniel was that "the saints of the Highest One will receive the kingdom and possess the kingdom forever, for all ages to come" (Dan. 7:18) and "the time arrived when the saints took possession of the kingdom" (Dan. 7:22). Thus, the Son of Man is identified with "the saints of the Highest One" (Dan. 7:18,22) who are under his domain (see Dan. 7:14), clearly indicating both a person and a group of persons— a community. Jesus understood that his mission was "to create the Son of Man, the kingdom of the saints of the Most High."[34]

> He was *more* than man but he was *man*. It was in him alone that the true destiny of man was achieved, and this was through suffering and death (Heb. 2:6-13). The mystical yet real solidarity between Christ and his people is such that not only is he the Son of man, but his people become in him the "Son of man."[35]

Individuals become his people when they respond through faith to Jesus Christ in order that the totality of his work of atonement may be wrought in them. To say that salvation is in Jesus Christ means "not only that our salvation comes from him, but also that it is due to the fact that we are brought into a vital relationship to him."[36] While Jesus during his earthly ministry did not command, exhort, or urge men, "Believe in me!" as far as specific words themselves are concerned, the fact of his calling men to commitment to or faith in himself cannot be denied. "In such phrases as 'Follow me,' 'Learn of me,' 'Forsake all and follow me,' there is a demand for faith in himself as insistent as Paul's words to the Philippian" [37] (see Acts 16:31).

The individual who is united with Christ then becomes a part of others, a part of a body like unto himself. Paul, following his statement concerning how men are saved (Eph. 2:8-10), moved on to use several concepts which are of a corporate nature to indicate the individual's status after salvation. He reminded them that they once were separated from Christ and at a distance but now, as believers, are part of Israel, heirs of the covenant, fellow citizens with the saints, in the household of God, a building built upon the foundation of the apostles for a holy temple and a dwelling for God (Eph. 2:11-22). This holy temple and dwelling place of God is the church, that is, "the saints who are at Ephesus" (Eph. 1:1), people who are identified as "His body— the body of Christ (Eph. 1:22-23; Col. 3:15).

The First-Century Christians

After the Holy Spirit came on the followers of Jesus in the upper room, they moved into the streets of Jerusalem to witness to the people gathered there from all over the world for the observance of Pentecost. Peter preached his message based on the prophet Joel and declared Jesus to them (Acts 2:1-36). The people were convicted and asked Peter what they could do.

As a result of the witness of the disciples and the preaching of Peter, Luke said, "Those who had received his word were baptized; and there were added [see KJV, *unto them*] that day about three thousand souls" (Acts 2:41). "The Lord was adding to their number day by day those who were being saved" (Acts 2:47). The increase is simply to the group of disciples who are not yet clearly seen as "the" church or "a" church.

The word *church, ekklesia* in the Greek, occurs in Acts for the first time as the story concerning the growth of the disciples of Jesus is told (5:11). *Ekklesia* is used at this point for the fourth time in the chronological sequence of the New Testament events. Jesus used the word once in Matthew 16:18, then twice in Matthew 18:17. Up until the first use of church in Acts, the followers of Jesus were known by several designations in the account by Luke—*apostles* (four times,

Acts 1:2; 4:33,35; 5:2), *witnesses* (Acts 1:8), *Men of Galilee* (Acts 1:11), and *Brethren* (Acts 1:16). They are referred to as *everyone* (Acts 2:43) and *their own* (Acts 4:23, the NASB supplies *companions* and the KJV *company*). The group at prayer identified themselves to God as his *bond-servants* (Acts 4:29). Then, for the first time in Acts *ekklesia* occurs—after the death of Ananias' wife "great fear came upon the whole church" (Acts 5:11).

Thereafter, the word *church* becomes a clear and much used designation for the followers of Jesus. However, it is not the only word, term, or idea used to identify these people in the remainder of the New Testament. Other phrases used are "body of Christ," "household of faith," "fellowship of the Holy Spirit," "fellowship of Christ," "fellowship of the Holy Spirit," "fellowship of Christ," "temple of God," "a spiritual house." [38] The use of the various terms with their own intrinsic and unique suggestions contribute to the fullness of the theological understanding of the church. No one of them totally captures the significance of the people of God but each is the people of God viewed from a special perspective which supplies the abundant and significant revealed truths about the church.

The witness of the one hundred twenty persons (Acts 1:15), the group made up of the twelve and other believers, produced a church in Jerusalem. The group of believers was added to (Acts 2:41,47), then, as previously stated, we find them designated as "the whole church" (Acts 5:11). While the idea cannot be dogmatically maintained, the possibility is very strong that in Jerusalem numerous groups of believers were meeting in various homes throughout the city. These "house-churches" comprised the totality of the church in Jerusalem.

As the work of witnessing by the disciples went on, the concept of specific, localized, individual congregations unfolded throughout the movement. After the conversion of Paul, Luke wrote that "the church throughout all Judea and Galilee and Samaria enjoyed peace, being built up; and, going on in the fear of the Lord and in the comfort of the Holy Spirit, it continued to increase" (Acts 9:31). The conclusion is very evident that all of the believers in these areas— Judea, Galilee, and Samaria—did not meet in one individual congregation but that the word *church* as used here is inclusive of all believers. Numerous local churches were necessary for the believers to worship, to fellowship one with another as Christians, to be involved in mutual upbuilding, to witness, and to minister.

Scattered by persecution, some believers came to Antioch (Acts 11:20-21); and as they proclaimed Jesus, a large number of people turned to the Lord. The church at Jerusalem (Acts 11:22) heard what had happened and sent Barnabas to Antioch. He, in turn, after arriving on the scene, went to Tarsus to engage Paul in helping him (Acts 11:23-25). Luke stated, "for an entire year they met with the church" (Acts 11:26). This is the first occasion in Acts where clearly in the context, without any possibility of a difference of opinion, there were two churches identified—one in Jerusalem (Acts 11:22) and one in Antioch (Acts 11:26). The separate identity of the church at Antioch is also clearly set forth (Acts 13:1-2) in God's instructions to it concerning his special work for Paul and Barnabas. The same truth is underscored in the report of the missionary pair after their first journey (Acts 14:26-27), as well as the fact that the church at Antioch sent them to Jerusalem to meet with the church and leaders of the church there to discuss the issue of circumcision (Acts 15:1-4).

Paul and Barnabas retraced their steps in Asia Minor to Lystra, Iconium, and Antioch, strengthening and encouraging the disciples in the area. They also "appointed elders for them in every church" (Acts 14:23). The words, "every church" indicates that more than one church had been planted by the men and that, possibly, there was a church in each of the cities named. The first occurrence of the word *church* in the plural occurs when Paul and his new companion Silas were on the second missionary journey. They traveled "through Syria and Cilicia, strengthening the churches" (Acts 15:41). Then, when Paul and Silas visited Derbe, Lystra, and Iconium and were reporting to the people the decisions of the Jerusalem Council, Luke said that "the churches were being strengthened in the faith, and were increasing in number daily" (Acts 16:5).

The inescapable conclusion is that there is a sense of spontaneity about churches coming into being in the book of Acts. Apparently the followers of Jesus did not deliberately plant churches but, rather as they witnessed, the Holy Spirit worked to create a community of believers. The testimony of the Scripture is that obedience to Jesus Christ in sharing his message of salvation inevitably and spontaneously brings into being the outward, external structure termed *churches,* which is an expression of that inner, spiritual reality that when an individual is saved he also is incorporated into a group of persons of all the ages who are the people of God; the body of Christ; "the spiritual-mystical church."

As Paul went, churches appeared throughout Galatia and in Corinth, Ephesus, Philippi, Colossae, and Thessalonica. Some unknown believers went faithfully witnessing and a church appeared at Rome. Some other unknown ones, or maybe the same ones, witnessed at Smyrna, Pergamos, Thyatira, Sardis, Philadelphia, and Laodicea, and there churches were born. The witness of faithful disciples produced churches. Clearly, in the New Testament, we observe church growth in terms of increase in the number of churches conforming to the idea, that church growth is produced spontaneously when the church functions day by day as a redemptive community.

Elements for a Strategy

While spontaneity comes through very clearly in the beginning of churches in the New Testament, still a sense of some deliberate plan of action also seems to be present. In that which these Christians were and which they did—whether it was done intentionally or unintentionally, whether it was a deliberate strategy or an unorganized plan of action—some elements for building a church planting strategy can be recognized because they were the element behind the planting of churches in the New Testament. Today these are significant for the strategists who plan for and the church planters who begin churches.

Some of these discernible elements for church planting were related to the Christians themselves, that is, who they were or the kind of people they were as God's people. They were a people of prayer, joy or gladness, conviction, determination, persistence, obedience, boldness, and flexibility. They were united in mind and purpose with a love for each other which was genuinely expressed in true fellowship. They worshiped, glorified, exalted, and praised God. They allowed God to lead them and use them by his Holy Spirit.[39]

Other discernible elements were related to methodology—that which they did or engaged in as a natural outflow of who they were. Because of who they were, they involved themselves in the worship of God and expressed their sense of fellowship with each other as fellow Christians in sharing the needs of physical life. In addition, they communicated the message of the gospel through preaching, witnessing, and teaching, as well as ministering to the physical needs and dealing with the problems of people. They involved other people in the work of the church both in the immediate area—the "deacons" in Acts 6, Paul to help at Antioch and elsewhere, and yet others to help in extending the gospel beyond the immediate area—John, Mark, Paul, Barnabas, Silas, Timothy, Luke, and others. They preached about Jesus, witnessed about what he had done for them, and exhorted people to make decisions. They took advantage of that which happened to them as opportunities to witness and even sometimes were so flexible that most inappropriate circumstances became opportunities to communicate the gospel. They preached and witnessed to people wherever they found them and sought a point of common ground or contact through which men might be open to the message.

The New Testament Christians somewhat reluctantly recognized the universal scope of God's work but did come to a final and clear conviction that the gospel was for all the peoples of the world. They realized that they needed to distinguish between cultural matters and the central core or truth of the gospel. They experienced circumstances that were for purging, cleansing, and refining through which they grew in their understanding of God's will and work. They strengthened, instructed, and disciplined the churches which they had planted. They monitored, supervised, and evaluated what had been accomplished in the spreading of the gospel through the efforts of the various workers. They went to major key cities and neglected no one as they reached out to the slaves of their times but also were alert to witness to significant people of political, social, cultural, educational, and economic leadership. They shared the gospel with all the various people in the communities where they went.

As the gospel was spread, the believers of the first century both contributed to the needs of less fortunate Christians and supported financially the further advancement of the gospel throughout the world. They confronted internal problems, such as a fellowship disturbance, the law/grace dilemma, and a leadership dispute and found solutions. They were harassed, oppressed, and persecuted but continued advancing the influence of God's people. They also abandoned the unresponsive and unproductive places.

Still other discernible elements do not fall easily into either of the above groupings but need to be noted. Two of these have to do with personnel and one with results. God used human instruments. The work done in the extension and growth of churches is, in the final analysis, God's work but it is done through people, not independent of people. Also, God used bi-vocational workers—men who provided for themselves all or a part of their livelihood. Finally, "God gave the increase" (1 Cor. 3:6, KJV). The churches grew in all areas. They grew as people who, knowing who they were, developed or matured spiritually, organized to do their best, followed a Christian life-style, and spread the influence of the churches so that not only did the churches increase in the number of members but the number of churches also increased.

H. E. Dana stated: "Even at the giving of the Great Commission the church was still in its incipient stage, for two vital reasons. First, it had not yet become a definite *reality in the consciousness of its constituency.* Second, it had not yet assumed any definite *modes of corporate life.*"[40] Through various experiences the church came to the point in its development of church consciousness so that "it was accepted by the close of the apostolic age as the dominant element in the promotion of Christ's redemptive movement."[41] In a similar way, the church also developed modes of corporate life so that it can be seen as an outward structure.

The overwhelming realization of being caught up in God's redemptive purpose was the primary motivating factor in the lives and actions of the Christians recorded in the New Testament. Out of this reality flowed an exciting, dynamic, captivating, vital spontaneity which is essential for Christian service and its accomplishment for the glory of God. However, elements of strategy—basic realities, intent, plans, procedures—were there. At the same time, these did not occupy the foreground. Just as the artist follows in a painting the laws which produce harmony, symmetry, contrast, and focus, these basic elements cannot be allowed to blur the image to be conveyed. The architect must plan well the framework for the building, but it is not seen. The strategy is significant but it is the framework for sharing the redemptive message of God which, when shared, produces Christians and churches because this is God's plan.

We should *be* Christians as nearly as is humanly possible. Through living, loving, and ministering as we ought as God's people, we incarnate the message of the gospel. However, the growth of the church is toward the end that the kingdom of God might be expanded into the lives of more people. The New Testament Christians went everywhere preaching the gospel and extending the call of God to the entire scope of human society, both the Jews and the Gentiles, the rich and the poor, the classes and the masses. As they did so, men and women responded, the kingdom of God grew, and local churches came into existence.

We, today, need to recapture the note of spontaneity which existed in the New Testament era and, therefore, produced churches as the believers witness to the Lord Jesus Christ. Church planting does involve specific and deliberate intent to start new churches, but the New Testament points to the fact that new churches and church planting are the direct and inevitable consequences of the believer's involvement in witnessing and proclamation. Everyone who is brought to an experience of salvation needs the worship, fellowship, and maturing that the church alone can provide so that he may fulfill his obligation to not only minister but also to be a witness in both deed and word to the grace of God. The church must be there to build up the individual Christian so that he in turn may communicate the message of salvation as he goes back out into the world.

God's method centers in the people of God—the body of Christ which edifies itself intensively so that it may in turn edify itself extensively in new members brought into the local body and also in new churches planted for the growth of the total spiritual body. We must keep before us preeminently God's plan—man, *and* churches because churches are people and are central in Christ's redemptive movement.

Notes

1. One major exception to this statement is William Owen Carver in his book, *Missions in the Plan of the Ages* (Nashville: Broadman Press, 1951). The original copyright was by Fleming H. Revell Company in 1909. The new terminology related to church planting is not present in his discussion, but many concepts are there in essence.

2. Ibid., p. 175.

3. Where Scripture references are given, although sometimes these may be numerous, they may not include all possible references. However, in most cases, only a few references to biblical texts will be cited.

4. The Bible presents, most people generally agree, eight covenants—agreements between God and a person or group of persons. Three of the covenants are general and, thus, apply to all mankind. These are the Edenic, Adamic, and Noahic. The other five covenants—the Abrahamic, Mosaic, Palestinian, Davidic, and New—are related to the special people of God.

5. Alan M. Stibbs, *God's Church* (London: Intervarsity Fellowship, 1959), p. 54.

6. Donald G. Miller, *The Nature and Mission of the Church* (Richmond: John Knox Press, 1957), p. 70.

7. The English words *choose, chosen, choice, elect,* and *election* occur forty-four times in the Scriptures. The Greek words translated by these English words are from three different Greek root forms. Two of these are from one Greek root; two from another, and the forty remaining words from the same root.

8. Romans 1:7. Compare also 1 Corinthians 1:2; 2 Corinthians 1:1; Ephesians 1:1 where the word "saints" occurs.

9. Richard C. Trench, *Synonyms of the New Testament* (Grand Rapids: Wm. B. Eerdmans Publishing Co., 1958) p. 331.

10. Walter T. Conner, *The Gospel of Redemption* (Nashville: Broadman Press, 1945), p. 194.

11. See for discussion and comparison, W. Robertson Nicoll, ed., *The Expositor's Greek Testament* (Grand Rapids: Wm. B. Eerdmans Publishing Co., 1967), V, p. 57; IV, pp. 196-197 and Marvin R. Vincent, *Word Studies in the New Testament* (Grand Rapids: Wm. B. Eerdmans Publishing Co., 1946), I, p. 644; IV, p. 346.

12. Trench, p. 367.

13. Nicoll, III, p. 270.

14. J. Robert Nelson, *The Realm of Redemption* (Greenwich, Conn.: Seabury Press, 1951), p. 11. Nelson's scriptural reference in a footnote has been incorporated into his statement.

15. Karl Barth, *The Knowledge of God and the Service of God* (London: Hodder and Stoughton, 1938), p. 151.

16. Karl Barth, "An Exegetical Study of Matthew 28:16-20," *The Theology of the Christian Mission*, ed. Gerald H. Anderson (Nashville: Abingdon Press, 1961), p. 64.

17. Ibid.

18. Paul S. Minear, *Eyes of Faith* (St. Louis: Bethany Press, 1966), p. 121.

19. Donald G. Miller, *The Nature and Mission of the Church* (Richmond: John Knox Press, 1962), p. 74.

20. Orlando E. Costas, *The Church and Its Mission: A Shattering Critique from the Third World* (Wheaton: Tyndale House, 1974), p. 89.

21. Ibid.

22. Ibid., p. 90 gives Costas' explanation of numerical, organic, and conceptual expansion and incarnational growth. He gives no reason, however, for the first three being identified as expansion and the last as growth.

23. Frank Stagg, *New Testament Theology* (Nashville: Broadman Press, 1962), p. 175.

24. Three different Hebrew words are used in these references. In the last three places cited from the Psalms, the same word is used. In both Jeremiah 23:3 and Psalm 23:2, the two words are different although they are related. The *New American Standard Bible* translates in each reference the two related words with the English word *pasture*. The King James Version translates the Hebrew word in Jeremiah with the English word *fold*. Both Hebrew words have the basic meaning of home, dwelling place, or habitation.

25. Stagg, pp. 172-173, where the same thought is set forth to explain or help to understand the use of *ecclesia* only three times in the Gospels (Matt. 16:18; 18:17).

26. Stibbs, p. 54.

27. Stagg, p. 175.

28. Walter T. Conner, *The Faith of the New Testament* (Nashville: Broadman Press, 1940), p. 159.

29. Ibid.

30. Archibald W. Hunter, *The Work and Words of Jesus* (London: SCM, 1956), p. 85.

31. Vincent Taylor, *Jesus and His Sacrifice* (London: The Macmillan Co., 1937), p. 282.

32. Ibid.

33. Walter T. Conner, *Revelation and God* (Nashville: Broadman Press, 1936), p. 165.

34. T. W. Manson, *The Teachings of Jesus* (London: Cambridge University Press, 1935), p. 227.

35. Stagg, pp. 60-61.

36. Conner, *The Gospel of Redemption*, p. 150.

37. Hunter, p. 88.

38. Paul S. Minear, *Images of the Church in the New Testament* (Philadelphia: Westminster Press, 1960). He wrote concerning the numerous terms for the church, "conservatively estimated, there are more than 80 of them, but this number might readily be increased to 100 if various Greek words were counted separately" (p. 29). See his book *Jesus and His People* (New York: Association Press, 1956). This small book covers some of the basic terms used for the relationship between Jesus and those who believe in him. It also has a list of additional terms not discussed, along with the biblical references.

39. The Bible references are not given here because they are so numerous. With a careful reading of Acts, and the epistles of the New Testament, and/or the use of a concordance, the scriptural citations can be found.

40. H. E. Dana, *A Manual of Ecclesiology* (Kansas City: Central Seminary Press, 1944), p. 74. See the entire discussion on pages 74-95.

41. Ibid., p. 75.

2
The Nature of Churches

Justice C. Anderson

What is the nature of churches? How can we distinguish between the kingdom of God, "the Church," and churches? Overall, how should we relate together these three biblical concepts? How are the three ideas related mutually one to another? What points of danger or error do churches need to be alert to in order that they might be used more effectively? What are the distinguishing realities about the church? Are these truths also valid for churches?

Justice C. Anderson is currently professor of missions at Southwestern Baptist Theological Seminary, Fort Worth, Texas. A native of Texas, he was graduated with a Bachelor of Arts degree in 1951 from Baylor University and with both the Master of Divinity degree in 1955 and the Doctor of Theology degree in 1965 from the seminary where he is now teaching.

He has served as the pastor of churches in Texas and as a missionary to Argentina for the Foreign Mission Board of the Southern Baptist Convention. He has written A Manual of Homilectics in Spanish, A Study of Baptist Ecclesiology in Spanish, *and numerous articles both in Spanish and English for Southern Baptist periodicals.*

You say, "Let's go to church." Is the church some place to go?

Another says, "My church believes such and such." Is the church an organization with bylaws?

You give money "to the church"; then the church must be those who collect and spend the money!

"I grew up in the church." What does that mean?

Still another may insist, "The church ought to do something about it!" What is this church that he thinks should act?

"At my church," opines another, "we have a great choir program." How can a church be *my* church? And is the church a place to have programs?

"We go to Dr. So-and-So's church," states someone else. Is it really Dr. So-and-So's church?

Others argue, "The church keeps up the moral tone of the community." Is that the business of the church?

"The best people in town belong to the church," we are told. Is the church, then, the society of the socially and morally acceptable? [1]

These commonplace sayings clearly demonstrate the multifarious meanings of the word *church.* Other popular concepts compound the problem of a precise definition. Without doubt, many never get beyond the idea of the church as a building! Like the fifth-century barbarians who coined our English word *church,*[2] the spatial concept prevails. The church is a place to pass by, get married in, or to have the preaching service. Others realize that the church is not merely a building but that it exists in the people and activities which go on in the building. To them the church is like a club, a fraternity, in which they can enjoy the company of some high type of people. Dues are required to keep the buildings and activities properly maintained. Closely akin is the view that the church is a social agency with humanitarian ends, in other words, the religious arm of the United Way to prevent cruelty to human beings! Along with this, many consider the church to be a clinic where personal problems are solved; or, put in another way, it is a type of religious physical fitness center where moral and spiritual jogging are prescribed to keep us religiously fit!

Another common view of the church is that it consists of those who come weekly to hear a great preacher. A gifted orator gathers about him a loyal following who so love to hear him speak that they would not miss an opportunity to hear him. Such "churches" tend to fade away rapidly when the dynamic personality moves away. Akin to this view is the idea that the church is a society to preserve the memory of Jesus. In other words, the church stands in the community as a monument to the past tradition of Jesus Christ and his mighty acts. Like the local museum, it perpetuates a great memory.

Now, how can all these be the church? Did Jesus have in mind buildings, clubs, officers, money collectors, and organizations when he said to his disciples, "I will build my church; and the gates of hell shall not prevail against it" (Matt. 16:18, KJV)? Of course not! The plain fact of the matter is that the New Testament confronts us with "a church" which is not any one of these or all of them put together. The biblical foundations of the churches presented in the preceding chapter lay the basis for the correct concept. And the quest for this correct concept is not just a meticulous academic exercise. Upon its successful completion depends the task of church planting. The birth of healthy churches depends on church planters who have a clear understanding of the nature of the church. In the hands of biblically uninformed church planters, who are analogous to unskilled midwives, the birth of a church can only result in unseemly abortion, tragic stillbirth, or uncalled-for deformity. The church planter must start with a conscientious attempt to understand the nature of the church. The purpose of this chapter is to suggest a theological basis for evangelizing and congregationalizing.

Thesis

The thesis of this chapter is that the nature of churches can best be understood in the light of the New Testament doctrine of the kingdom of God. In other words, the planting of churches (local congregations) will be spiritually enhanced and doctrinally undergirded when viewed from the perspective of the New Testament concept of "the spiritual Church" [3] and its relation to the "coming Kingdom." Viewed thusly, the task of local church multiplication (or planting), sometimes considered to be the provincial and pragmatic achievement of "baptized behavioral sciences," is enhanced by universal and eschatological dimensions which are basically biblical. It is my belief also that New Testament congregations need to see themselves as "extenders of the Kingdom" and "members of the spiritual Church of Jesus Christ." This provides a certain theological dignity for church growth theory which is sorely needed.

The best way to extend the kingdom of God is to build up the church of Jesus Christ by multiplying local churches, in other words, the reproduction principle. Baptists and many other Evangelicals have been too individualistic and materialistic about this whole matter. They major on the winning of individual souls and the construction of larger buildings to put them in! There has been an evangelistic introversion which is basically centripetal. This is what Peter Wagner calls "the syndrome of church development." [4] The organized congregation is considered an end instead of a means. Energies formerly invested in outreach are diverted into well-intentioned efforts to direct the inner spiritual and organizational growth of the church. The local church is seen as an induction center for religious devotees instead of a training camp for lay witnesses. Pastoral care and Christian nurture are not meant to *replace* evangelism; they are intended to *supplement* it. Many of our local churches are like certain young couples who pay an exaggerated amount of attention to their new baby, allowing their own lives to become much too involved with the child. The ultimate loser is usually the overly coddled child. As in the case of such couples, one of the best ways to solve the problem is multiplication—have another child! Let the congregation give birth to another.

I think Hans Hoekendijk was right when he entitled his book, *The Church Inside Out*[5]—the inside must be going out in order to avoid the threat of institutionalism. It is wrong to conceive of church and mission as two distinct entities; speaking about the church can only be meaningful in the context of speaking about the kingdom of God and the whole world. The Church, therefore, is essentially missionary or she is not the Church. The true nature of the local churches will dissipate without their being drawn outside of themselves by the magnetic, biblical doctrines of the spiritual Church of Jesus Christ and the eschatological kingdom of God.

This should not be strange to Southern Baptists, who in the constitution of their Convention are very careful to protect the autonomy of the local church, but who correctly add,

> It is the purpose of the Convention to provide a general organization for Baptists . . . for the promotion of Christian missions at home and abroad and any other objects such as Christian education, benevolent enterprises, and social services which it may deem proper and advisable *for the furtherance of the Kingdom of God.*[6]

It is this "furtherance" which I wish to emphasize as a key to the proper understanding of the nature of our churches. Although given token mention in our confessions of faith such as *The Baptist Faith and Message,*[7] I fear that the evangelical Baptist masses really don't comprehend it. If the Baptist and, I think, New Testament emphasis on the local congregation is to result in church reproduction,[8] it desperately needs the widening effect of "a universal stretch" and the lengthening effect of "an eschatological pull." This stretch and pull creates a healthy theological tension which dignifies church extension. The churches see their true nature when they consider themselves a part of the spiritual church and as agencies of the coming kingdom. As Doran McCarty says,

> Whatever happened to the Kingdom of God? . . . Is it possible that those of us who are North Atlantic theologians . . . could regain the sense of the Kingdom of God and enrich our theologies . . .? Until Christianity recovers the dynamic of showing the world a sense of hope that God is working in the future of our world, we cannot expect to recover a sense of militancy, loyalty, and dynamic.[9]

Definition of Terms

Having presented some popular misconceptions about churches and having presented the "kingdom concept" as a possible corrective, it is necessary to analyze more closely some of the terms we have already used. A clear understanding of the terms "the kingdom of God," "the church," and "a church" [10] is crucial in the quest to comprehend the nature of churches.

The Kingdom of God [11]

What is meant by the "kingdom of God?" What is its relation to "the church" and "the churches"? A local congregation must see itself in the light of the kingdom. The kingdom of God involves the whole notion of the rule of God over his people and particularly the vindication of that rule and people at the end of history.[12] Simply stated, the kingdom of God is the rule of God as it relates to persons, to peoples, to societies, and to history. The notion of *a people of God,* called to live under the rule of God, begins in the Old Testament and with it the notion of the kingdom of God. Peter Beyerhaus states it succinctly, "The Kingdom of God is God's redeeming Lordship, successively winning such liberating power over the hearts of men that their lives and thereby finally the whole creation become transformed into harmony with His divine will" (Rom. 8:21).[13] This is the reason why the kingdom of God could never be established by political or moral action. The kingdom presupposes a miraculous change of heart which God himself initiates. It requires a radical renewal of the mind (Rom. 12:1).[14]

A true New Testament, local church must understand its nature from the vantage point of the kingdom. Even when it calls itself a "free church," it means that it is free to be subject to a theocracy. It also carries the burden of "kingdom citizenship" which implies a regenerate membership and a social responsibility.

The idea of the kingdom permeates the whole Bible although the term as such is mainly found in the Gospels. This is due to the fact that for Jesus the supreme concern was the kingdom of God. "He saw the Kingdom as that degree of recognition of the holiness and righteousness of God on earth as will cause the reign of God to include the earth in his realm even as heaven is his kingdom." [15] Directly or indirectly, all the parables of Jesus have the kingdom for their subject; for most of the parables this is their express purpose. From the first of his ministry (Matt. 4:17) to the last (Matt. 26:64), Jesus' thoughts moved in the circle of "the kingdom concept."

We should know that the founder of the church conceived it in the light of the kingdom. His church is not *all* of the kingdom, but it is definitely a significant part of the *becoming* kingdom. He saw his church as a vital part of the *missio dei* (the mission of God). In turn, according to the Bible, the *missio dei* has as its purpose the revelation of God's kingdom and the restoration of his liberating rule. He reached his most trying experiences trying to correct the misconceptions of even his most devoted disciples. This is why he had to mention the kingdom one hundred and ten times and the Church only twice! He felt an understanding of the nature of the kingdom would ensure the correct nature of his church and its churches.

The problem of the kingdom is still with us. Men still have trouble interpreting it. Some say it has to do only with the inner life of the individual, with the rule of God in the heart of man. Yet, while the kingdom of God is doubtless of determinative importance for the inner life, this was not the only concern of Christ. Others relate the kingdom of God exclusively to the Church, so as practically to identify the two. *Basileia* and *ekklesia* are vitally related but separate concepts. Still others view the kingdom of God solely in terms of the fulfillment of man's spiritual needs and the forgiveness of his sins. Yet, nowhere in the New Testament is the kingdom of God spiritualized or defined in this way. As an announcement and realization of salvation, the kingdom has to do with the totality of human needs.

The kingdom of which the New Testament speaks has an incomparable depth and richness. It has dimensions which embrace heaven and earth, world history and the universe (see Col. and Eph.). The kingdom of God is the new order, which began in Christ and which will be completed by him, wherein all relationships will be put right; and not only that between God and man, but also those between people, nations, sexes, generations, and races, and even that between man and nature. It is this of which the prophets of Israel spoke. This is the meaning of the visions in the book of Revelation. And it is this of which the apostles testified when they spoke of looking forward to new heavens and a new earth where justice dwells (2 Pet. 3:13). J. H. Verkuyl expresses it like this,

> The Kingdom of God is a redeemed creation, the victory over chaos, the abrogation of all anti-messianic tendencies and the completion of God's liberating work. This Kingdom has come in Jesus Christ and will be brought to completion in and by him and his Spirit. If this is God's purpose, then it is *this message of the Kingdom which must be the frame of reference and point* of orientation for mission.[16]

The birth of a church takes on sacramental sanctity when seen from this perspective. The mission of church planting and multiplication is in the first place that of inviting men to know Jesus as the Lord of a kingdom.

In summary, the kingdom is present and future; here and coming.[17] The eschatological pull of this dynamic force should be the incentive for church growth; its universal presence should be the motor for ministry (Matt. 6:9-10). As John Bright says,

> The New Testament Church is the people of the Kingdom of God. And that Kingdom is even yet "at hand," intruding into the earthly order. We can enter that Kingdom, can obey its bidding, can witness to its power, can pray for its victory, can (God help us!) steel ourselves to suffer for it. But we cannot escape its tension. For it is a Kingdom that we can neither create nor abandon—and remain the Church; It is ours, therefore, to find again, now in this time, the New Testament tension. Perhaps if we do so, we may be approved as good and faithful servants.[18]

The Universal Church

In the aura of the kingdom concept, we are prepared to discuss the nature of the Church in the world. Up to now we have used interchangeably the terms, "the Church" (with a capital letter) and "a church" (with a little letter). Now we would like to make a distinction. The New Testament doctrine of the church includes both the specific, local, organized entities—"the church which was in Jerusalem" (Acts 11:22), as well as the total body of all believers of all ages and places—the use of the imagery of the physical body and marriage in Ephesians and Colossians. The latter has been referred to as the universal, glorified, triumphant, and invisible church. These words are used to encompass the total redeemed body or the assembly of all believers of all ages and every place, although they are never in a group with close physical proximity until the redemption of the believers is completed in the presence of God. In other epistles Paul dealt with the church in its practical, functional relationships but in Ephesians and Colossians he viewed it in its relationship to Christ himself and its nature as a spiritual entity. Therefore, in these epistles the word *church* is used "to represent spiritual Israel [and] . . . is hence purely a spiritual conception, connoting a mystical followship of the saints and relationship to Christ." [19]

Words as vehicles of concepts or ideas always confront us with the difficulty of semantics. No one word captures the totality of the richness of thought in the context of Scripture where this "spiritual-mystical" reality about the totality of all the redeemed is expressed. Each word because of its varied uses is full of thoughts that are not intended. *Universal* is good in that it expresses the common heritage of all believers in all ages but poor in that it has been used as a worldwide form of structure or organization. *Invisible* is an attempt to state the spiritual reality, yet believers are not beings who cannot be seen. *Glorified* or *triumphant* expresses the eschatological destiny of the church but is out of touch with present reality. Possibly the words *spiritual* or *mystical* if properly understood are better words to express the idea of "the Church" and this will be interchanged with the word *universal* which even when use herein is emptied of all ideas of organization and structure.

The nature of a local church can only be understood in the light of the New Testament doctrine of the spiritual Church. This Church existed before and makes necessary the churches. A brief perusal of the use of the word *church* (*ekklesia*) in the New Testament reveals this fact. The word is used approximately 114 times in the New Testament. Five references refer to the classical meaning of a physical assembly, usually political. These uses have nothing to do with the New Testament Church. Approximately 90 times *ekklesia* refers to a physical assembly of believers in Christ—what we would call a local congregation. For this reason, the majority of Baptists and free churchmen have emphasized the local church, the church as a congregation. However, we must not forget that the word is used in a metaphorical sense 19 times where it refers to a spiritual-mystical community of all the believers in the world.[20] Many Evangelicals have neglected this use since it has been so abused by certain Catholic traditions. Along with the frequent use of terms such as "the body of Christ," "the family of God," "the people of God," and others which can refer to this same body of believers, this metaphorical use is very significant and should not be ignored. It is necessary as a proper context for the existence and the understanding of the local congregation. Without it as a background, the local church can easily lose its divine dimension. This spiritual-mystical Church plus the kingdom concept form the backdrop for a clear understanding of the nature of a local church. They also enhance its importance. They give it a universal significance which prevents ethnocentrism and provincialism.

Having already addressed ourselves to the nature of the kingdom, let us attempt a definition of "the Church": "the fellowship of believers in Jesus Christ in the world, a spiritual and redemptive community, whose unique institution is a local church, and whose purpose is the extension of the Kingdom of God." [21] This is the idea of "the Church" as a world community of believers, a spiritual organism, which only organizes and institutionalizes at the local level. It can never come together in a physical assembly. Nevertheless, it is a present reality "in the world." It is present and seen. This is why I have never liked the phrase "the invisible church." When a believer has his experience with Jesus Christ, he becomes a member of "the Church." Then he is ready to become a member of "a church." He really cannot understand the nature of "churches" until he sees them in the light of "the spiritual Church."

This spiritual-mystical Church is closely related to the kingdom but not identical with it. As Peter Beyerhaus says,

> Jesus introduced some new elements to an understanding of the Kingdom of God: its focus on Himself, its spiritual reality, and its emphasis on the creation of the new community. (1) The Kingdom proclaimed in the New Testament evangelism is centered in Jesus Christ. (2) It is a Kingdom realized by spiritual regeneration. (3) It leads into the Church as the new messianic community of the Kingdom.[22]

Our "free church" fear of centralization and ecclesiasticism should never drive us to ignore this predominant New Testament doctrine. It greatly enhances the place of a local church as we will illustrate later. The kingdom, already discussed as a starting point in our quest to understand the nature of churches, presupposes a messianic community. This community is the metaphorical Church alluded to previously. It is "the people of God" destined to exercise a messianic ministry to the rest of the peoples (Matt. 24.12). The Church is in the world to hasten the establishment of the kingdom. Notice I did not say "to bring in the kingdom," That is God's prerogative or that it will be an earthly kingdom, since evidently the kingdom is always coming and must be understood eschatologically. However, Dr. W. O. Carver thought that more "earthly emphasis" should be given to the kingdom. He felt the churches were failing when they neglected the "nowness" of the kingdom.

> We do not preach and pray for the coming of the Kingdom of God on earth, at least not yet; nor in any anticipated time. Thus our evangelism seeks to enroll people for the heavenly home when they shall no longer be able to retain place or find a home anywhere on earth . . . Does not our "evangelism" consist far too largely in seeking to induce men to accept the grace of God to provide an entrance ticket to the glory of a future heaven, while we do not dare proclaim the ethical demands of the Kingdom of God here and now?[23]

The nature of this spiritual-mystical Church is illustrated by the biblical figures of the body and bride of Christ, the household of God, the temple, or the vineyard of God. However, these are metaphors which throw light on our definition. An analysis of the above definition reveals two key elements: the Church as *a people* and the church as *a community*. These are the two poles of the biblical reality of "the church." The "people of God" concept is common to both Old and New Testaments (Ex. 19:5-6; 1 Pet. 2:9). The Greek word for "people" is *laos*, from which comes the Latin *laicus* and the English *laity*. This reminds us that the whole Church is "a laity," a people. The constituency of "the Church" is God's people scattered throughout the world. Here the point is *universality*. If the local congregations we have, and plan to plant in the future, do not start with this universal concept, they run the great risk of provincialism. "The churches" are the agents of "the Church" which, in turn, is the foretaste of the coming kingdom. Seen in cosmic-historical perspective, the Church is the "people of God" in hundreds of specific denominations, movements, and other structures. It is a people, not an organization. It is a community, not an institution. However, its basic structure is "a local church" congregated voluntarily. Before moving on to see the nature of "a local church," two other aspects of "the Church" must be mentioned: the Church as the "body of Christ" and the Church as the "temple of the Holy Spirit."

The Church as the body of Christ speaks of corporate unity. The believers are all present in Christ. He is the fountain of our lives, and we are the instruments of his will. It is in this context that we see the catholicity and the apostolicity of the church. The catholicity of the body is seen in the elimination of all national, racial, and sectarian barriers. "A church," or a denomination must be cognizant of this fact (Gal. 3:28). Orlando Costas points to another ramification of this concept,

> The Church is also catholic in that it permits men and women to be themselves in their anthropological fullness . . . it embraces men of all cultures . . . it enriches their respective cultures, gives greater depth to their talents and abilities, and restores them to fuller humanity." [24]

The apostolicity of the Church means that she is the "sent one." She must never become a "folk-church" or a "territorial church," or even just "a local church." She must not become *too* indigenous! As Christ's special agent she has been sent forth to represent him in every sphere of human existence (John 20:21; 2 Cor. 5:20).

Thirdly, the Church is not only the "people of God," "the body of Christ," but also the "temple of the Holy Spirit." This simply means the Church will be indwelt by the Spirit of Christ. Jesus took the place of the old Temple concept of the Jews. The Temple was the place where God and man met. They met most perfectly in Jesus Christ (John 4:20-24). Thus, Christ becomes the new temple of God. The Holy Spirit is the spirit of Christ (Rom. 8:9; 2 Cor. 3:17). Therefore, the Church is the temple which the Holy Spirit indwells. Wherever the Spirit is, there is Christ and his Church.

Therefore, "the Church," as it has been treated here, is the earthly agent of world evangelism and reconciliation (Eph. 3:10). This spiritual community is in one sense the kingdom "in formation" in space-time history before the return of Christ. God's plan is to be accomplished through this Church. The birth of New Testament congregations and their subsequent multiplication needs the purifying biblical breezes of the New Testament doctrines of "the kingdom" and "the Church."

The Local Churches

Having established the proper background, it is now possible to define "a church." This is the predominant concept in the New Testament. Since the word *ecclesia* is used in this sense ninety times, Baptists and other evangelicals have placed their major emphasis here. When we speak of the planting and multiplication of churches, or the task of congregationalizing, we are referring to local congregations. These local congregations are the concrete manifestations of the spiritual Church. They are operational bases of the kingdom. This is why *The Baptist Faith and Message* gives them priority.

> A New Testament church of the Lord Jesus Christ is a local body of baptized believers who are associated by covenant in the faith and fellowship of the gospel, observing the two ordinances of Christ, committed to His teachings, exercising the gifts, rights, and privileges invested in them by His Word, and seeking to extend the gospel to the ends of the earth.
>
> This church is an autonomous body, operating through democratic processes under the Lordship of Jesus Christ. In such a congregation members are equally responsible. Its Scriptural officers are pastors and deacons.[25]

Then it comes to recognize "the spiritual Church idea" in a final, brief sentence: "The New Testament speaks also of the church as the body of Christ which includes all of the redeemed of all the ages." [26] Although the order is different, this document is saying that the local and the universal must go together in order to be true to the New Testament. As Dr. H. E. Dana says,

> Were the misinterpretation of this New Testament term merely a matter of literary inaccuracy we might afford to pass it by. But it is more. It involves an erroneous conception and consequent misapplication of one of the most important elements of Kingdom progress; namely, its organization. History has rendered it incontrovertibly certain that the form of organization in the Kingdom of Christ tremendously affects the attitude of the individual believer toward him, and influences the practical efficiency of the Gospel . . . A wrong conception here may wreak havoc in the whole program of kingdom extension.[27]

No one is going to find in the New Testament a *detailed* description of how to organize or structure a church. However, we Baptists, along with other Evangelicals, believe that the norms are sufficiently clear to speak of a New Testament ecclesiology. In other words, "the churches" are "the Church" in organized, local form. The multiplication of such "churches" is the way to extend the kingdom. We can define "a church" as,

> a local community of Christians voluntarily congregated, correctly baptized, and biblically organized, which meets to worship God, observe the ordinances, and under the direction of the Holy Spirit carry out the Great Commission of Jesus Christ at home and abroad.[28]

Because of its great influence in Evangelical circles today, and particularly because of its emphasis on the "multiplication of local churches," a word must be added about the Church Growth School of Donald McGavran and his followers.[29] All of the significant missionary conferences of the last twenty-five years have been influenced greatly by this missionary ideology. Starting on the foreign mission fields, the Church Growth Movement has come home to these United States.[30] In short, the Church Growth School emphasizes the numerical growth of churches. The quantitative expansion of congregations is the first priority. All other phases of work must be made subordinate to the purpose of multiplying churches. For this purpose, it makes use of people-movements among the so-called "homogeneous units" of societies such as tribes, castes, social, and economic classes. This aspect amounts, in fact, to the establishment of ethnically-constituted churches. This school develops a strategy to pinpoint responsive populations and then concentrate resources on them. It plays down the importance of resistant areas. Missionary research must discover the methods which yield successful church growth or the factors which retard such growth. The behavioral sciences are heavily depended on to help in this analysis.

As one can see, these principles are concerned with the multiplication of local churches. However, many are questioning their validity in the light of what we have said about the kingdom and the universal church. Can "churches" grow to the point that they grow out of their proper nature? Can "churches" cease to be members of "the church"? I am reminded of a warning paragraph I found on a can of "Real-Kill Weed Killer" which said, "After application, weeds sprayed may flourish for a short time. The ingredients force the weed to grow so fast that the whole plant dies!" This is what worries me about the Church Growth School's methodology. It's so effective that it could kill the whole plant!

Perhaps the Church Growth School needs a stronger emphasis on the kingdom concept. The overall influence of the school has been beneficial to the mission of the church. Any missionary program concerned with the multiplication of congregations should study it and profit by it, but certain objections have to be made in the light of Christian theology in general.

The quantitative should not be separated from the qualitative. The true New Testament nature of the churches will be concerned with both, with what we might call organic growth. Also, the emphasis on numbers and responsive areas seems to negate the prophetic element of the churches. There will always be an important place for "outpost missions" in resistant, unproductive areas. If we were to abandon small, oppressed churches, which humanly speaking have no chance of growth, in order to direct our energy to the "winnables," we may, as J. H. Verkuyl says, "find ourselves the object of the complaint of the voice from Gethsemane: 'So you men could not keep watch with Me for one hour?'" (Matt. 26:40).[31]

Also questionable is the theory that the caste, tribe, and class are the best vehicles for the spread of the gospel. Certainly the churches do not want to be instruments of ethnocentrism, tribalism, or new caste systems. May we attempt to achieve church growth along ethnic lines at the cost of isolating the members of the body of Christ? It is true that men like to become Christians without crossing racial, linguistic, or class barriers. However, the gospel must challenge ethnocentric prejudices and practices. It should not confirm the givenness of local beliefs and practices. It must include a note of judgment and repentance in anybody's culture. The Church Growth Movement definitely subordinates the prophetic task to that of social conservation.[32]

Akin to this is the one-sided way of setting priorities according to response. In the Bible the priorities are more flexible. They change from situation to situation. Sometimes it's the fight against hunger, at other times the struggle for justice, and at others, the proclamation of the gospel. What is needed is a holistic approach which is flexible enough to respond to God's guidance.

Again, this school tends to separate the spiritual from the socioeconomic-political complex. The Bible knows nothing of this type of separation. The school also views the church solely in terms of its relation to God. It gives secondary attention to the Church and the world. The larger theological questions of the gospel, the nature of the Church, and the kingdom are neglected. In spite of these weaknesses, the Church Growth School's concern for the multiplication of local churches has contributed much to the revival of emphasis on the local churches. Southern Baptists have much to learn from Dr. McGavran and his disciples. His utter commitment to church multiplication and his evangelical sincerity compensate for his strong claims and his alleged theological weaknesses or oversights.

In summary, this section of our study has emphasized the importance of the kingdom of God and the spiritual Church for a correct understanding of the nature of the churches. Its thesis has been that the best way to extend the *kingdom* is to build up *the Church* by multiplying *churches*. However, the precautions mentioned above must be considered. Local congregations should not be proliferated at the cost of kingdom characteristics such as universality, historicity, and eschatology. It is time now to sum up and briefly analyze the characteristics of "the church" of our Lord Jesus Christ as it is seen in the "churches."

Characteristics of the Church/Churches Complex

When Jesus Christ said to Simon Peter, "Upon this rock I will build My church; and the gates of Hades shall not overpower it," he referred to what I have described as "the Church." He was not thinking about a local church at this point.[33] In this context he connects his Church to the kingdom when he said, "I will give you the keys of the kingdom" (Matt. 16:17-18). This is the biblical spawning ground for the local church idea. Out of this organism which was spiritual, universal, and communitarian came the organization which was local and institutional. The local church is the universal church in miniature. It is an agent of the kingdom. The general characteristics we are going to isolate refer to the "Church/churches complex." They refer to the Church as the body of Christ. His body was our temple when he was on earth; now his Church is our temple since his resurrection and ascension. God now tabernacles among men in Jesus, and Jesus lives in his Church. In reality, this church we are going to describe, be it in the spiritual or the local sense, "is the community of the resurrection, the fellowship of men in whom God's Spirit dwells, the fraternity of the forgiven, the people who are called out of the world to belong to God, in order that their corporate life may consist in his worship and service." [34] It is this "Church," which includes "the churches," which I want to characterize.

First, *the church* [35] *is divine in its origin.* It is not a human accomplishment. In one sense it is a divine-human institution, but the divine initiated it. We receive the church from God; we certainly do not gather it up. The free church tradition runs the risk of humanization with its emphasis on "the gathered church." Let us remember *who* does the gathering. The church is not a religious club created by a group of religious men. It was created by God through the resurrection of Jesus Christ. Church growth and planting can never be the automatic result of applying human effort; modernization of methods are simply means by which the church expresses itself.[36] The new thrust of Southern Baptists to congregationalize must take this into account. The ultimate success will depend on the gracious work of God and not the efficacious work of man. A church is always a gift of God. Our primary task is to examine whether we are proliferating "the Church" through the multiplication of "churches." Are the con-

gregations being formed aware that they are integral parts of the
Church of Jesus Christ? Does the nature of the local church reflect
the characteristics of "the Church"?

Secondly, *the church is corporate in its constitution.* The term *membership*
must be recaptured in its pristine purity. To be in Christ is to be in
the Church. The Church is an organism from which each member
draws his life. The word *corporate* (Latin *corpus*) reflects this. We are
the many in one. The church is not a bouquet of believers or a collection of individual Christians brought together by mutual agreement.
The church is not a conglomerate but a community. Never is one
less of an individual than when he exercises personal faith in Christ.
By that very act of faith, he is identified with Christ. He becomes a
part of the body. When we join "a church" we are witnessing the
fact that we are already a part of "the Church." Our faith is personal
but not individual. Through it we become personally ingrafted into
a corporate reality. Just as a body is not made by collecting a hand
here, an arm there, a foot somewhere else, and then putting them
together, so the church is not made up of isolated individuals. This
act of faith which sets us in Christ, sets us in the *society* of Christ.
The churches are the visible entities of this spiritual society. Our
independence and autonomy should be tempered by this act.

Thirdly, *the church is a fellowship in its community.* It is not essentially
an organized institution. It does not consist of buildings or programs
but of people. No one structural form of institutional life, or any
specific form of worship, is the *essence* of the church. The church is
certainly not a hierarchy of clergy who dispense grace to laymen.
Different members have different functions, but no one person or
group of persons is the church. The church is the body of believers
who are "in Christ." The natural leaders should be allowed to rise
to the different functions; but the corporate fellowship idea should
be predominate.

Fourthly, *the church is universal in its scope.* It *is not* local but manifests
itself locally. The local church, therefore, is not *a* church, it is *the*
Church at that place. A local gathering of Christians is Christ, the
whole Christ, present and making himself known there at that point.
(1 Cor. 10:17; Rom. 12:5; 1 Cor. 12:12-27; Heb. 12:23; Eph. 1:10)
Due to the barriers of time and space, all believers cannot be present
when the church meets. However, a local church is a part which is

equal to the whole because each part possesses not a fragment of the Christ but the whole Christ. We should not be less diligent in multiplying congregations; but in doing so, we should realize that the Church is not merely the particular congregation to which we belong or the denomination to which it adheres. When one unites with a congregation in a particular place he unites with the spiritual, which is a universal Church. This spiritual church is not made up by adding all local congregations together. The whole church is present in any local congregation. It is the whole people of God looking out on the world at that point. It is like a window in a house, a place to look in and out. This idea gives a universal note to church-planting which prevents provincialism and encourages missionary outreach.

Fifthly, *the church is an organism in its function.* It is not just an organization. It is a spiritual organism, not a carnal organization. A church, no matter how finely organized it may be, has no existence unless the Spirit of the living Christ lives in her now. A church is not some kind of a mummified museum which serves as a memorial to the past. A church is the living communicator of the living Lord. It is only as he lives *now* in a church, that a church *is* the Church. This organic growth is important. "One cannot dogmatize too much about the criteria for a healthy church, for a growing church is like a sensitive plant reacting to its local soil and ecological conditions. It must be understood *organically* and not institutionally or administratively." [37] This is why numerical growth cannot be the only criterion. Orlando Costas [38] says that church growth should be "holistic." His definition involves four dimensions of growth or expansion. First, numerical expansion. Second, organic expansion which has to do with the internal development of the community. Third, conceptual expansion or the degree of consciousness that a community of faith has with regard to its nature and mission to the world, to its Scriptures, to its image in the world. Fourth, incarnational growth is the degree of involvement of a church in the life and problems of her social environment (Luke 4:18-21). Most of our Baptist local churches are somewhere between the second and third dimensions. However, in the light of the kingdom concept, the congregations we spawn should be four-dimensional from the start. This brings healthy growth and avoids the syndrome-of-church-development already mentioned.

Sixthly, *the church is expendable in its purpose.* In other words, it is a means to an end. The kingdom is the end. The church exists for the glory of the King. Therefore, worship becomes one of its main reasons for being. Worship should not be selfish. It is not what we receive from it, but what we communicate to God. Consequently, the outlook of the church is not toward her self-preservation but toward the salvation of the world. We often mention "going" and "sending" as vital parts of the mission of the Church. We do not mention "dying" as another part! As Christ had to die to save the world, the church must be constantly "willing to die" to fulfill her mission. Insofar as a church exists merely for the sake of serving its own members or meeting the needs of a select few who have banded together for mutual betterment, it ceases to be the church. As Donald Miller says,

> The church is an army, committed to the sacrifice of self, engaged in costly action in God's warfare against evil, looking forward to that day when the kingdom of the world has become the kingdom of our Lord and of his Christ, and he shall reign for ever and ever (Rev. 11:15).[39]

The local churches which we plant must be self-giving from the first. They want to get out of themselves into their own propagation and service projects. They will not want to passively receive all the time; they will desire to actively serve others with what they have.

This perusal of the true characteristics of churches indicates that the popular conceptions in the mind of many are far wide of the New Testament conception. The time is overdue when the churches should rethink the meaning of their existence—especially, those who want to participate in the birth of new churches. These characteristics emerge when we see our churches in the light of the kingdom.

Aberrations

The concept of church planting in the light of the kingdom of God is not without its dangers. History reveals many aberrations with reference to the nature of the church. A return to this "Kingdom-Church-churches complex" as the key to the right theology of church planting can be grossly misinterpreted. The mention of a few historical errors may serve as warnings to us.

First, there is *triumphalism*. This is identifying your church or your denomination with the spiritual church or the kingdom of God. The classical example of this is the Roman Catholic Church which for many years held to this viewpoint. In the first place, it is not right to identify "the Church" with the kingdom, much less *your* church! This leads to sectarianism and religious despotism. Even some Baptists in certain moments of the Landmark Movement moved close to this error. This is the threat of exclusive denominationalism. It can easily move over into this aberration. Strong or large local churches can commit this error—a crass institutionalism which pretends to have an hegemony over others or to triumph over them. Our intention to multiply churches should not have the sole purpose of building up *our* denomination or even our local church; it should result in the furtherance of the kingdom.

A second aberration is *ethnocentrism*. This is to identify the church and the kingdom with your race or your culture. It believes that those of other races or cultures are not only different but wrong. It identifies the church with a general ethnic group and tries to perpetuate Christianity in the name of that group. Certainly the kingdom of God and his universal church can never be forced completely into one's culture.

A third error is *humanitarianism*. This is elevating the social, economic, and even ecological concerns of the kingdom to a place of prominence, while relegating proclamation, evangelization, and church planting to a secondary position. All these things are important in kingdom work. The kingdom comprehends the whole man and the whole universe. For this very reason the spiritual aspect of man must have prime importance. The church should always respond to human need. It should seek to liberate the oppressed and alleviate the poverty of our world. However, this must not be done at the cost of the other. Proclamation, evangelization, and church planting must be the priorities without neglecting the other.

A fourth error is *materialism*. This is bringing the kingdom down to earth and confining the church to a place. "My kingdom is not of this world," said Jesus (John 18:36). He had this problem with his disciples. They wanted to mix his kingdom up with the kingdom of Israel or the Temple in Jerusalem. This is why he talked so much about the nature of the kingdom. He was constantly trying to explain it. His modern disciples have the same problem when they equate church growth with buildings and programs.

A fifth aberration is *individualism.* This is personalizing the kingdom. It wants to contain the kingdom in the individual heart. It has no social concern at all. It talks about personal salvation, forgiveness, and a heaven out there in the future. It imprisons the kingdom and the church in the heart of the individual. The collective sense of the kingdom is reserved for heaven or for the future end of the world. This is characteristic of Western psychology. It makes a church just the sum total of souls who mutually agree to form it. There is no sense of the corporate.

A sixth error is *chiliasm.* This is to identify the kingdom with a political entity or nation. In church history since Constantine, religion and politics have been all mixed-up. A state is interpreted to be the people of God. Usually this state is thought to have a bearing on the future of the kingdom which is coming to earth in a millennial age. Israel had trouble with this. Since her time other states and political entities have tried to put themselves in the place of the Church as the agent of the kingdom.

A seventh error is *institutionalism.* This is to substitute a club, a society, or even a local congregation for the church and the kingdom. A particular institution of the kingdom tries to usurp the place of the kingdom! Even an evangelistic association, a church growth movement, or a denomination can do this when they try to absolutize their work or structure.

Positive Products of the Kingdom Concept

In conclusion, let us briefly look at some positive products of the thesis of this chapter. First, the "kingdom concept" brings a sense of *majesty* to the birth of a church. What could be a busywork program of church planting, when seen from this perspective, takes on a sense of awe and wonder! Having understood the true nature of the churches he is planting or developing, the worker and the members are under the spell of the King. Their endeavor is God's endeavor. Their efforts are already crowned with victory. In the final analysis, the results do not depend on them. They are subjects of the King participating in kingdom work. Their efforts are tied to the end of things. The evaluation of their work awaits the end of the ages.

A second positive product is *authority.* The church planters' proclamation and work carries a note of authority. They are acting in obedience to the command of their Lord. Theirs is no common task which runs the risk of human venture, theirs is a holy task which has the aura of divine adventure! This authority breeds a certain reckless security which pushes them out into new areas of conquest for the King.

A third product is *universality*. Their parish is the world. The kingdom is universal. Their church is a part of the spiritual universal Church. Therefore, the mission of their church is universal. The modern missionary movement developed out of this concept.

A fourth product is *urgency*. The presence of the kingdom in the world creates a constant crisis, a holy and healthy tension which forces churches into feverish redemptive activity. The eschatological factor contributes to this also. The King is coming again. The very nature of the churches in the light of the kingdom emits a sense of urgency.

A fifth product is *contingency*. The church is not dependent on a place. It is mobile and flexible. Its programs and emphases are contingent upon the working of the King in the world. Its constants are able to be communicated in many different forms. Innovation, originality, and creativity are encouraged. The old and the new are important to the kingdom. (Matt. 13:52) The people of the kingdom are in constant exodus. They do not depend on the fading and transitory structures of history. The gates of hades cannot prevail against this versatile church which manifests itself in so many churches.

A sixth product is *actuality*. The kingdom is now and tomorrow! Therefore, the church of the kingdom is not just a memory; it is a present reality. It is a dynamic force. It is growing like the mustard seed; it is bringing in the catch like the fisherman's net; it is leavening the world. It is fresh and contemporary. This is the nature of a church which sees itself related to the kingdom. It is working faithfully in the present with an eye on the future.

A seventh product is *spirituality*. The kingdom church has a sense of mystery to it. The drawing power of the unknown is there. The sovereign Spirit of God is in control. There is never a dull moment. There is a sense of spontaneity which only the Spirit can bring. What does the Spirit of the Lord say to the churches? is the constant question. And the same Spirit gives gifts and power for the task of the church.

These are some of the products of churches who understand their

nature, who see themselves as windows of a world Church which is
the coming kingdom.

Conclusion

It is heartening to see the revival of interest in evangelism and
church planting among Southern Baptists. The Home Mission Board
is marching under its twofold banner of "evangelizing and congregationalizing." The Foreign Mission Board is emphasizing the importance of "the establishment and multiplication of indigenous
churches." Our seminaries are branching out into theological education by extension. Outreach is the order of the day. However, all
will be in vain without an underlying, biblical knowledge of the nature
of churches. I have proposed the dynamic and unifying idea of the
kingdom of God as a key to open the meaning of the nature of the
churches. I believe that the biblical doctrine of the kingdom should
continue to be the motivating force of the living Church and its
churches. Church planting and reproduction are the priorities of the
day. However, the motivation for this great task must spring from a
kingdom consciousness. A quote from the late Max Warren is an
apt way to sum it up:

> The essence of the new life for the Christian lies in this—that his
> entire present existence is lived in the fellowship of the Kingdom which
> is to come. Our very expectancy that in and through the events of
> our time God is at work, fashioning His Kingdom, is for us a hope
> born of our experience in the fellowship. *That fellowship in turn realizes
> its own nature* in proportion as it looks towards the future, knows itself
> to be the 'becoming Kingdom,' God's particular providence at this mo-
> ment in history, pledge of his unchanging purpose to save all mankind.[40]

"For Thine is the kingdom, and the power, and the glory, forever.
Amen" (Matt. 6:13).

Notes

1. Although not a direct quote, I am indebted to Donald G. Miller, *The Nature and
Mission of the Church* (Richmond: John Knox Press, 1959), p. 9 ff.

2. For the whole etymological background of this see H. E. Dana, *A Manual of Ecclesiology* (Kansas City: Central Seminary Press, 1944), pp. 13-22.

3. The term *spiritual church* means the universal community of believers, sometimes called the *invisible church*. I would really prefer the term *universal church* which shows its catholic or ecumenical nature. However, in many Evangelical (and especially Baptist circles), the words *universal, catholic,* and *ecumenical* carry connotations which make them counterproductive!

4. Peter Wagner, *Frontiers in Missionary Strategy* (Chicago: Moody Press, 1971), p. 169.

5. J. C. Hoekendijk, *The Church Inside Out* (Philadelphia: Westminster Press, 1966).

6. Clifton Allen, ed., *Annual of the SBC, 1975* (Nashville: Executive Committee of SBC, 1975), p. 30.

7. The document, after a long definition of the local church, adds, "The New Testament speaks also of the church as the body of Christ which includes all of the redeemed of all the ages" *The Baptist Faith and Message* (Nashville: The Sunday School Board of the Southern Baptist Convention, 1963), p. 13.

8. See the *Guide for Establishing New Churches and Missions* published by the Home Mission Board of the Southern Baptist Convention (Atlanta: Department of Church Extension, 1977), p. 1. The Home Mission Board has coined the word, "congregationalize," which I hope will come to be commonly used among Southern Baptists.

9. Doran McCarty, "A Theology of Culture and Its Implications for Mission," an unpublished paper delivered to the Doctor of Ministry Colloquium at Southwestern Theological Seminary, October 18, 1976.

10. Throughout this chapter I will use the word *Church* with a capital letter to refer to the spiritual or universal church, while the word with a small letter will refer to a local church or congregation.

11. There are other terms in the Bible which refer to the kingdom. It is not mentioned as such in the Old Testament, but it is implied in all the Old Testament message.

12. John Bright, *The Kingdom of God* (Nashville: Abingdon Press, 1953), p. 18.

13. Quoted in Paul Little, ed., *Reaching All* (Minneapolis: World Wide Publications, 1974), p. 13.

14. Unfortunately, some so-called "renewal movements" today have neglected this biblical aspect of renewal.

15. W. O. Carver, "Jesus' Problem with the Kingdom of God," *The Review and Expositor* (Vol. XLVI, No. 3, July, 1949), p. 300.

16. J. H. Verkuyl, "The Purpose and Aim of Mission" (unpublished Van Dyke Lectures at Calvin Seminary, July 21-23, 1976).

17. Bright. The whole book gives a complete study of this concept.

18. Ibid., p. 243.

19. Dana, p. 56; see his entire discussion, pp. 51-66.

20. Justice Anderson, *"Estudio de la Palabra Ekklesia"* (unpublished study written in Buenos Aires, Argentina in 1961 in Spanish).

21. Quoted from a handout given to basic missions classes at Southwestern Baptist Theological Seminary by Justice Anderson. It is his own definition occasioned by his first real confrontation with Roman Catholicism in Argentina in 1960 and its concomitant idea of "The Catholic Church." This is a New Testament missionary definition.

22. Little, pp. 13-14.

23. Carver, p. 305.

24. Orlando Costas, *The Church and Its Mission* (Wheaton: Tyndale House, 1974), p. 27.

25. *The Baptist Faith and Message,* pp. 12-13.

26. Ibid.

27. Dana, pp. 23-24.

28. Author's own definition printed in class handout.

29. The school originated in the 1950's. See Peter Wagner's book *Your Church Can Grow* (Glendale, Calif.: Regal Books, 1976), pp. 10-12 for a good summary of the history of this school.

30. The USA branch of the movement is called the Church Growth Institute and is led by Win Arn.

31. Verkuyl, pp. 33-34.

32. In all fairness, it must be mentioned that the "homogeneous unit" is seen as a method to reach people initially and congregationalize them. Dr. McGavran then moves on to the idea of "bridging" which makes necessary the breaking out of the original mold.

33. I feel that Jesus here referred to the community of believers, not to a local congregation. However, the local idea is present in the generic sense. More definitely Jesus makes necessary "the local congregation" when he spoke of the church in Matthew 18:17.

34. Miller, p. 16.

35. Remember that the universal idea of the church is being indicated by the word *Church* and the local idea by the word *church.*

36. "The question is how far church growth can be processed through computer-like methods. One senses an element of determinism in calculating the relation of cause and effect which only remotely fits the actual empirical situation where results are frequently unpredictable and an open-ended approach must be taken," James Scherer, "The Life and Growth of Churches in Mission" in Gerald H. Anderson and Thomas F. Stransky, *Mission Trends No. 1* (Grand Rapids: Wm. B. Eerdmans Publishing Co., 1974), p. 171.

37. Ibid., p. 175.

38. Costas, pp. 89-90.

39. Miller, p. 20.

40. Max Warren, *The Truth of Vision* (London: Canterbury Press, 1948), pp. 62-63.

3
The Purpose of Churches

W. Bryant Hicks

Why are churches in the world? Does their purpose relate to their being—their nature? How are they to be involved with men? Can churches place time or space restrictions on their purpose? Can churches restrict their purpose for existence to only certain people? Can they limit themselves in purpose to only certain segments of mankind or to certain areas of a man's life? What means are available to churches so that they might fulfill their purpose? Is church planting related to the purpose of churches?

W. Bryant Hicks is associate professor of Christian Missions and World Religions at the Southern Baptist Theological Seminary. A native of South Carolina, he was graduated with the Bachelor of Arts degree in 1947 from the University of North Carolina. He was also graduated with both the Master of Divinity degree in 1950 and the Doctor of Philosophy degree in 1956 from the seminary where he is now a professor. He has done postdoctoral study at Union Theological Seminary in New York City.

He has served as assistant pastor and pastor of churches in Kentucky and as a missionary in the Philippines for the Foreign Mission Board of the Southern Baptist Convention. He has written various articles for Southern Baptist periodicals.

The purpose of churches can be properly understood only in light of the purpose of God for his creation. Ephesians (1:6,12,14) clearly sets forth the intention of God for his people that whatever they do should be for his glory. Verse 6 indicates that we are predestined for adoption as sons according to the intention of God's will "to the praise of the glory of His grace." In verses 12 and 14, again it is expressed with regard to his purpose and the end to which he is moving, that it should be "to the praise of His glory." The basic understanding of what the "glory" of God means in the Bible is that it is his very nature and being. His glory is not something that is added to him from the outside, but rather a demonstration of who he really is. To glorify God is to show what God is like by the life that we live. Jesus Christ speaks along the same line, "Peace be with you: as the Father has sent Me, I also send you" (John 20:21). In this statement, which is first expressed in John 17 in his high priestly prayer and then directly to the disciples themselves in chapter 20, the Lord indicates that his disciples are to be concerned with the same things that were paramount in his purpose.

This purpose is expressed in various Scriptures but perhaps especially in Ephesians 3:11. Here, following a statement that the mystery hidden for ages has now been revealed in the day of Christ and that this was in order that the manifold wisdom of God should be known through the church, the declaration is made, "This was in accordance with the eternal purpose which He carried out in Christ Jesus our Lord." Not only does this purpose include the redemption of all mankind but it also includes the "summing up of all things in Christ," as expressed in Ephesians 1:10. These are the broad purposes of God for his creation.

As we consider, then, the purpose of churches, we begin with the awareness that it is to be in keeping with the purposes of God in Jesus Christ which he has made known through his life here on earth. Perhaps it would be helpful to think of this task which God has given to his people under three basic headings: intentions, extent, and means.

The purpose of churches, then, is intended first of all for God's glory. Even in the Great Commission of Matthew 28:19-20, the mandate for missions is based on the fact that all authority in heaven and earth is given to Jesus Christ. On this basis the command can be given to go and make disciples of all nations. If the churches have as one of their intentions to glorify God, then they must always act in keeping with God's nature as made known supremely through Jesus Christ. The churches must never cheapen the gospel in any fashion by becoming hucksters of the truth, an activity against which the apostle Paul strongly warned. No matter how much of a stumbling block the cross may be, for example, God's people must never be guilty of preaching a gospel in which there is no cross, both the cross of Christ himself as the crucified Lord and the cross of the believer as he is to be crucified with Christ (Gal. 2:20). Jesus himself indicated that the way people would be drawn to him effectively would be in his being lifted up upon the cross.

Many who have engaged in personal witnessing have discovered that the cross has a tremendous attraction. There are those who are offended by the cross and who shrink from it, but very seldom do persons see the love of God in Christ made known on the cross without being wonderfully aware of how magnificent the love of God is for them. It may be that they have not been interested at all in prior discussions involving our faith and our theology; but when we point to Jesus Christ as crucified love upon the cross, people feel a strange and wonderful compulsion to respond to that love. Sometimes, of course, they resist, in spite of the attraction of the cross; but seldom does the confrontation take place without their feeling a compelling magnetism within it.

The second intention which God has set forth for his people is that of making disciples. In the Great Commission, the imperative verb in the Greek language is the one which is translated "make disciples." There are many things which we are expected to do as disciples of Jesus Christ, but it is eminently clear that all those who have become followers of Jesus Christ are expected, in turn, to seek to make disciples of others. The term *disciple* means one who is a learner or follower of another. It is not said that we are to go and save people but that we are to seek to make disciples of them. Consequently, as members of the body of Christ, we are to seek by every legitimate means to cultivate people and encourage them to become disciples of Jesus Christ.

Seeking to help others become disciples of Christ is not the most popular thing to be involved in nowadays. After all, people are often already actively involved in some sort of religious group. Many persons feel that to encourage such an adherent of another faith to become a disciple of Jesus Christ involves bigotry and intolerance. There is no question that this can be the case, depending upon the attitude of the one who is seeking to disciple another for Christ; but this is not necessarily so. We can be very loving, caring, and accepting of the other person at the same time that we are seeking to introduce him to Jesus Christ. If we want him to be open to our sharing and witnessing, we must be willing to be equally open to his sharing.

We have nothing to fear; for if what we believe is the truth and if
Jesus Christ is God's supreme self-disclosure in human form, then
this truth will triumph. As Charles Finney used to say, "The truth
is like a lion. You don't have to defend it; all you have to do is
turn it loose and it will take care of itself."

The really clinching factor in considering the matter of bringing
a person of another faith face-to-face with Jesus Christ in the hope
that he will become the Lord's disciple ought to be found in the
sheer fact that God himself saw fit to come in Jesus Christ to his
own covenant people, the Jews. If their being religious were enough
and if his self-disclosure through the prophets and through his mighty
acts of redemption were sufficient already, it is difficult to understand
why it was important for him then to make himself known in a clearer
and more compelling fashion through Jesus Christ. This should indicate to us without question that it is urgent that everyone in all the
world should know Jesus Christ. That is why this task of evangelism
and world missions is at the heart of our discipleship in Jesus Christ.

In the third place, it is God's intention that we be obedient to
his will. Our Lord indicated in the Great Commission that, when
we have made disciples, we are to teach them to obey all that he
commanded us. Notice, it does not say simply that we are to teach
them the content of our faith but that we are to teach them in such
a way as to encourage them toward obedience. This is an oft-neglected
intention of God for his churches. In Luke 6:46 Jesus had some very
stern words to say to his followers about this matter: "And why do
you call Me 'Lord, Lord,' and do not do what I say?" The same
kind of expression is found in Matthew 7:22, where the Lord said,
"Many will say to Me on that day, 'Lord, Lord, did we not prophesy
in Your name, and in Your name cast out demons, and in Your name
perform many miracles?' " He then told them to depart, for he never
knew them.

It isn't enough, then, for a person to have faith in the Lord. First
of all, there are many kinds of faith, such as superficial faith or shallow
faith. Then there is also faith which does not endure to the end, an
indication that it was not truly saving faith in the beginning. Most
evangelical Christians are very familiar with the famous "faith salvation" concept in Ephesians 2:8-9 and can quote this passage. Unfortunately, many of these same persons are not aware of verse 10, which

speaks eloquently of the importance of good works. It is true that we are saved by the grace of God through our response of faith, which as Holy Spirit he inspires within us. It is also true that this salvation is not a result of our good works, so that no one will be able to boast about achieving salvation. But verse 10 speaks explicitly to say that one who has truly come to know Jesus Christ as Lord and Savior is also going to be one whose life is filled with good works. Just as God chose Abraham and the Israelites for the purpose of blessing all nations and not just that they themselves might be blessed, in the same fashion we are saved by our faith response to God in Christ, not simple that we might be happy and enjoy life of an eternal quality but that our lives may be characterized by good works in obedience to the example and command of our Lord himself.

It is important to understand one more thing about this obedience: It is not to be slow-footed or grudging. Some church members, though they serve the Lord faithfully, manifest a spirit of reluctance during the very time that they are carrying out their acts of service. Oftentimes they will even complain about how hard it is to be a Christian and how unreasonable the demands are which are made on them. Of course, it may be true that unreasonable demands are made on members of churches at various times, for everyone knows that a willing horse will be worked almost to death. But the kind of people in view here are those who, overburdened or not, simply do not find the joy and fulfillment and satisfaction in their life of service which our Lord intends them to enjoy. Even Isaiah understood that religion is supposed to be a lift rather than a load, a boost instead of a burden. He says, "Bel has bowed down, Nebo stoops over; / Their images are consigned to the beasts and the cattle. / The things that you carry are burdensome, / A load for the weary beast. They stooped over, they have bowed down together; / They could not rescue the burden, / But have themselves gone into captivity" (Isa. 46:1). Then Jehovah cries out to the house of Jacob, "Listen to me, O house of Jacob, / And all the remnant of the house of Israel, / You who have been borne by Me from birth, / And have been carried from the womb; / even to your old age, I shall be the same, / And even to your graying years I shall bear you!" (Isa. 46:3-4). Here God makes it clear that he is not like the gods of other nations who must be borne around on the people's shoulders in order to protect the gods against the enemy. Rather, he bears his people around and sustains them from their youth all the way to their old age.

A fourth intention of God is that we are all to have abundant life. In John 10:10, the Lord cautioned his disciples that the thief comes to steal and kill and destroy. He then contrasted his purpose by saying, "I came that they might have life, and might have it more abundantly." This is another way, perhaps, of speaking about eternal life, which is so central in the teachings of our Lord and the early church. The apostle Paul spoke eloquently of the contrast in different words (Rom. 6:23). The Son of God came, then, not simply in order that persons might be alive but that they might have abundant life, which has something of the quality of the life of God within it.

It is not enough, therefore, to understand the salvation experience as simply deliverance from hell or as acquittal in a law court. There needs to be, in addition to that, the growing sense of the presence of the life of God within us. We want people to know conceptual truth insofar as we are able to help them to discover and understand it. But the churches must never lose sight of the fact that the real truth is Jesus Christ himself and that he is the one whom people must know if they are to have life eternal. This is what Jesus meant when he said, "You shall know the truth and the truth shall make you free" (John 8:32). A person can study theology, become well versed in it, and be able to discourse upon it with some authority and understanding without really knowing Jesus Christ himself personally. Our knowledge of doctrine or of truth generally is obviously and clearly inadequate as a means of discovering the abundant life, for this can be found only in a relationship of commitment and faith towards Jesus Christ.

These, then, are the intentions of God in relationship to his churches. These are the ends toward which he has directed us. Come next to a consideration of the extent of God's purpose for his church. First, it can be said that God's purpose extends to the end of the earth. Jesus said to his disciples, "But you shall receive power when the Holy Spirit has come upon you; and you shall be My witnesses both in Jerusalem, and in all Judea and Samaria, and even to the remotest part of the earth" (Acts 1:8). There has been a good deal of helpful discussion in recent years to the effect that a proper understanding of the purpose of God and his church is not primarily geo-

graphical. This is certainly true, especially if one is tempted to understand the West as the home base and all the rest of the world as
the mission field. Rather, we need to come to a more inclusive understanding which sees the home base of missions as wherever the church
has been established and the mission field as anywhere that Jesus
Christ is not being shared in fullness.

Such an understanding, however, must never cause us to forget
that there are still areas of the earth (such as Yemen) where virtually
whole populations of people live without ever having heard the gospel
of Jesus Christ at all. Among still other large groups of people (even
in the United States) the gospel has been presented in some fashion,
but only on a very shallow basis, and seldom in a face-to-face or
personal way. God's people must never be satisfied until the gospel
has been brought into the lives of people in every part of the earth,
at home and abroad, in a meaningful and sustained way. A proper
understanding of Acts 1:8 must never see these as being sequential
in nature. We must not see our involvement in missions as always
moving first of all to Jerusalem and then to Judea and Samaria, and
only then out into the rest of the world. These must be going on
simultaneously at all times. Some of the greatest and most needy
mission fields of our own day are areas of the world which in past
centuries were strongly Christian (as far as church membership is
concerned) but are now solidly Muslim, Communist, or simply indifferent.

There is inevitably and repeatedly an instinct in the mind of some
that makes them feel that we cannot do very much by sending representatives to other areas of the world to share the gospel as long
as we ourselves are so unfaithful here in this part of the world. Some
years ago a student came rushing into my office with the statement
that he had had a brilliant inspiration that he wanted to share with
me. I indicated to him that I was always eager to hear new ideas
and that I would like to have him share it with me. He then outlined
his plan, which consisted of bringing all of our foreign missionaries
back home to the United States, stationing them in large cities and
other areas that were so much in need of changing. Later, when all
of these difficulties had been straightened out and America was what
it ought to be, then, he said, we would be able to send our missionaries
overseas to other countries in good conscience.

The difficulty with such an idea is obvious. First of all, there is the assumption that by increasing the professional personnel here in the United States, we could guarantee that eventually our country would become substantially more what it ought to be. Such an idealistic assumption is not justified in any way by a consideration of the Scriptures. The people in other areas who have not heard the gospel have a right to hear it now, rather than having to wait until affairs have been straightened out in another part of the world. Someone has said that no one has a right to hear the gospel twice until everyone has heard it once. This is clearly an oversimplification; but there is a real germ of truth, namely that it isn't right for us to have such vast resources for sharing the gospel in our own country while these resources are so severely limited in so many other parts of the world.

In the second place God's purpose for his churches extends to the end of time. There is no indication in any word of Scripture that God's people are to seek his glory, disciple the nations, or bring abundant life to them through Christ only for a certain epoch of time. Rather, it is clearly assumed that this task will be carried forward as long as the church itself exists. As a conclusion to the Great Commission, Jesus said "Lo, I am with you always, even to the end of the age" (Matt. 28:20). Thus our Lord was saying that it is the task of the churches to see that the gospel is thrust into every part of the world in every age. This is a never-ending task, for, even where the church has been firmly established, it is within one or two generations of extinction at every moment. If this present generation of Christians does not reach out with the gospel to bring new people to faith in Jesus Christ, then the church will end at the death of all of those who now are Christians. A congregation can fall into the trap of being self-serving, but this does not mean that it is illegitimate for them to be concerned about their continuing existence. This obviously must never run counter to their standing firmly upon the truth of Christ or involve their compromising the clear self-disclosure of God through Jesus Christ.

The importance of continuing to reach out with the gospel to bring new people to discipleship in Jesus Christ as long as time exists was clearly indicated in the life of a congregation several years ago. This group of people was serving the Lord in a very wonderful way through many types of action ministries. They were moving out in all kinds of ways to help people with various needs in their lives. In fact, though the congregation was really very small, they were doing far more in ministry to the lives of others in that large community than dozens of other congregations put together. Their pastor repeatedly commented about the wonderful way in which these people were pouring themselves out in service to others.

At one juncture, however, he began to share with them his concern that they were not bringing anyone to know Jesus Christ as Lord and Savior. In fact, there was no overt indication in report or in conversation that they really had that as a major concern in their ministry. Lovingly, the pastor began asking searching questions. What would happen if they continued to minister year after year as they were doing at that time? Suppose they continued to minister until, one by one, they departed this life. At the end of that time, who would be left to minister to those who were living there at that time? This is not in any way to imply that ministry is not legitimate in and of itself; it is rather to insist that it is urgent for us in serving others always to keep in focus that we are followers of Jesus Christ and that we are not simply to "give . . . a cup of water" (Mark 9:41). The cup is to be given in the name of Jesus Christ with the genuine desire that the one to whom the cup is given will have the joy of coming to know Jesus Christ as personal Lord and Savior.

In the third place, the extent of God's purpose for his churches is to the end of humankind. As stated in the Great Commission, we are to make disciples of all nations or ethnic groupings. This is why we can never be satisfied simply because the gospel has been introduced into the general area of most of the nations of this world. There are many tribal or ethnic groups and many subcultures within larger cultures which still have not been effectively reached with the gospel, some of them not at all. Only in 1976-1977, for example, were the Giryama tribe of Kenya reached by a systematic, carefully planned, prayer-bathed witness that resulted in several hundred small congregations. Even when we think about a particular tribal group or national entity, we can never be satisfied until we have been as faithful as we can be to help in bringing the gospel to every last one within that group. The Lord certainly does not hold us responsible for the response which is given to our faithful sharing of the gospel, but he does expect us faithfully to dispatch our responsibility in seeing that every person has an adequate opportunity to be confronted with the claims of Jesus Christ upon his life.

That is why we must not be satisfied to use indirect methods alone in seeking to reach people for Jesus Christ. There are persons all around us in our own communities, and in other communities within our country, who have never had a really warm and caring presentation of the gospel made to them. They have seen the billboards and the advertisements. Perhaps they have even heard an occasional television presentation of the gospel, but they have not had the opportunity of sitting with someone who really cares for them and who lovingly leads them to realize their need of Jesus Christ. The magnitude of this task cries out for the involvement of all of God's people in seeking to fulfill it. There may have been a time when the faithful clergy and a few deeply committed church members would be able to carry out the task of evangelism in our communities. Such a time as that has passed off the scene long ago if it ever existed at all. People are so much on the move today and are so effectively insulated from a clear confrontation with the gospel that it is absolutely necessary that everyone who knows Jesus Christ seek to share him with those who do not yet know him.

The fourth element in the extent of God's purpose for his churches is that it should be to the end of human existence. In Matthew 25:31 ff., the Lord spoke about the last day, in which the sheep will be gathered on one hand and the goats on the other. There is no more chilling contrast than that between these two groups of people. Verse 34 speaks of those to whom the King will say, "Come, you who are blessed of My Father, inherit the kingdom prepared for you from the foundation of the world." To those on the left, on the other hand, he speaks words to chill the soul, "Depart from Me, accursed ones, into the eternal fire which has been prepared for the devil and his angels" (v.41). The Lord very clearly explained that the difference between the two groups will be determined by whether they have visited the sick, fed the hungry, clothed the naked, and helped the stranger. He went to the extent of saying that if we fail to do these things for those who are in need, we have failed to do it to him. For those of us who have grown up in a tradition which has emphasized salvation almost as if it took place in a vacuum, these words are somewhat troublesome. Yet it needs to be understood clearly that concern for such matters as these is at the heart of the gospel.

In the very beginning of his ministry, our Lord identified himself as being deeply involved with people concerning every need in their life. (Luke 4:18-19, read from Isa. 61:1-2). Clearly, these verses indicate the concern of our Lord for the poor and downtrodden, in both a spiritual and material sense. When the disciples of John the Baptist came to Jesus and wanted to know if he were really the Messiah, the proof that Jesus sent back to John by them was that the gospel was being preached to the poor. Wherever Jesus found people in need, he moved to fulfill that need, whether it was food, as in the case of the 5,000 by the lake, or sight for the blind.

This ought to settle in our minds the question as to whether we are to be concerned about people's eternal destiny or whether we are to be concerned about their human existence at the present time. The simple answer is that Jesus seems to have dealt with people in terms of their wholeness as persons. Whatever the need was, Jesus sought to satisfy it. Since he has sent us in the same way that the Father sent him, we ought to let him be our model and respond to people in the same way that he did. Some years ago it was assumed by some Evangelicals that their responsibility extended only to concern for a person's eternal destiny and that they need not be involved at all in seeking to help that person with his social or material needs. More and more we are coming to realize that such a separation of needs is artificial and, in some sense, impossible.

We have considered the intentions which God has for his people. We have also dealt with the extent of God's purpose for his churches. We now turn to the means which God intends for us to use in accomplishing this purpose. First of all, it is clear that the Lord intends to accomplish his goals in this world through the church. The writer of Ephesians indicated (in ch. 3) that grace was given to him to preach to the Gentiles the unsearchable riches of Christ and to make known the stewardship of the open secret which formerly was a hidden mystery. He then goes on to say that this was done "in order that the manifold wisdom of God might now be made known through the church to the rulers and the authorities in the heavenly places" (Eph. 3:10). In the next verse, he ties this in with the "eternal purpose which he carried out in Christ Jesus our Lord." It is through the church, then, that the Lord intends to accomplish his purpose that the mystery which has now become an open secret should be made known to the principalities and powers in the heavenly realm. It is true that God works other than through his church, for Paul himself indicated that even the created order bears witness to the true nature of God (Rom. 1:20); but the purpose of God in bringing all things under Christ always involves the church as the agency for sharing Jesus Christ.

This has not always been understood. Through whole segments of the history of the Church, God's people did not seem to understand that it was his intention that it should be through them that the gospel would be made known to all people everywhere. One of the biggest problems that came to the Reformed churches was at this very point. In the development of the life of the Church up to the Reformation in the early sixteenth century, it was the monastic orders that provided the missionaries in the life of the Church. It was almost as if the bulk of the people who made up the Church understood themselves to be in no sense involved in missions at all.

Then, when the Reformers were thrust out of the Church and began to take various segments of the Church in new directions, they reacted against many abuses within the life of the Church as it had been. One of the things that they did not like was the monastic system, so they simply rejected it. The difficulty was that, in rejecting the monastic orders, they also rejected the missionary stream in the life of the Church from which they had departed. Even William Carey, when he sought to bring missions into the life of the Baptist churches of his day, was looked at with a jaundiced eye and was told that God would save the heathen when he was ready and did not need the help of William Carey. The result was that missionary activity became the responsibility of a small group of people outside the life of the Baptist churches.

We can rejoice that, in the life of a number of denominations in the United States, missions has been understood to be the responsibility of the whole church. The mission agencies have not been understood to be separate societies comprised of interested individuals who would assume responsibility for carrying out missions. Unfortunately, however, in far too many congregations, missions has been relegated to a corner in the life of the group and has been fostered by only a handful of the members. There needs to be a new birth in our day of the understanding that the entire church is responsible for missions. We have all been sent on mission by the Lord into this world to carry out his task of reaching all people near and far. To whatever extent missions is understood in our congregation to belong only to a group of enthusiasts, to that extent the life of that congregation is limited. There is evidence in our day that more and more people are coming to understand that no congregation can be vitally alive if it is not functioning as an arm of the Lord's mission in this world: (1) seeking to involve all members of the body in mission activity in their own community, (2) praying for the Lord to call out some persons to go beyond their own territory, (3) giving sacrificially in order to send these beyond their territory, and (4) praying in an earnest and informed manner for those who are sent.

A second means through which God seeks to accomplish his purpose for his churches is that of service. We have already seen how Jesus has set the pattern for us in a life of selfless, sacrificial service for others. He did so in supreme fashion on the cross as he somehow dealt with our sins, once and for all gaining the victory for us. This should be the pattern for every congregation in our day around the world. One of the constant frustrations which church staff members and lay people alike face today is how to get people's attention. How can we break into their consciousness so that we will be able to present the claims of Jesus Christ to them? The answer to this seems to be found largely in following the example which Jesus Christ himself has given for us.

This has been demonstrated over and over again in places as far apart as Worcester, Massachusetts, and Forks of Elkhorn, Kentucky. In both cases the pastor led in discovering ways whereby he and his fellow Christians could minister to people in their needs. With joyful abandon they utilized all the resources in their fellowship, and many from the community itself, in helping people to discover how their various needs could be met. In the process they naturally came into a sustained relationship with many persons. This afforded them the opportunity of sharing their Christian faith with these persons, numbers of whom came to know Jesus Christ as their living Lord.

Any congregation who is busy reaching out in love to meet the needs of people in its community will discover that there is an almost inevitable and natural opportunity to point people to Jesus Christ and to give personal witness of what he means in its life. This kind of concern has sometimes been understood as ulterior in its motivation. If the service that we are rendering to people is understood to be solely for the purpose of getting an opportunity to witness to them, then this may be properly understood as ulterior in some way. However, it is not an ulterior motive when we minister to people because of their tremendous needs socially and economically and then take opportunity that presents itself to share Jesus Christ with them. In fact, this would actually seem to be a higher motive, for in doing this we are treating the person not as a mere animal but as a being who is in the image of God and who can relate to this wonderful Lord of the universe.

A third means through which God's purpose for his churches is fulfilled is the work of his own Holy Spirit. Luke records the words of the Lord Jesus as he counseled his disciples to tarry in Jerusalem until they were "clothed with power from on high" (Luke 24:49). Jesus seemed to be saying here that he did want them to be his witnesses in all the world but that they could not be effective witnesses until God as Holy Spirit moved into their lives in fullness. Thus he seemed to warn them against a brash, human aggressiveness or over-confidence. Nothing can more greatly hinder the effectiveness of God's people in carrying out the purposes which God has given to them than the assumption that the work can be carried out in mere human energy, wisdom, and ingenuity. Anytime a group of people begins to feel that all they have to do is plan their work and work their plan in order to accomplish their mission, they are in real trouble. It is the nature of the church that they must sow in hope and that they cannot predetermine what the harvest will be. This means that there is not room for arrogance or fear or anxiety as we labor faithfully for the Lord. Paul himself was wonderfully aware that he was not the one who brought the increase. He could plant and Apollos could water, but only God could bring the harvest. This is pictured very beautifully in John 15 when the Lord set himself forth as the vine and declared that we are the branches. It is significant to remember that the branch does not strain and strive in order to bring forth fruit. What Jesus declared as necessary is for the branch to remain in the vine (John 15:5). Here is a clear indication from our Lord that it is not enough for us to be faithful in terms of effort and activity.

It is also essential that we remain in close and intimate fellowship with him throughout the entire process, both in preparation and during the time of the activity and service themselves.

A growing chorus of Christians today bears eloquent testimony to the futility of a life in which the warm and vital relationship of God as Holy Spirit is not integral to service. It is a tragic thing to see so many faithful church members working almost frantically to bring in the kingdom. In no sense is this intended to say that God's people do not need to be busy; it is rather to say that busyness can be essentially empty if it is done in the energy of human effort, forgetting that this is God's mission and God's ministry in which he has allowed us to be involved and for which he enables us. Home and foreign missionaries and many faithful church members have shared recently out of their experience in which they were grimly serving the Lord, trying their best to be faithful in ministry and witness, yet aware that something was missing at the very heart of the matter. God was faithful and there was even some fruit; yet there was the clear realization that something was wrong, something lacking. Gradually they began to discover that they had forgotten that they were not servants *for* the Lord but that they were co-laborers together *with* Christ. The Lord does not commission us and then send us out in the community while he stays back at headquarters. Jesus, after commissioning all of us in Matthew 28:19-20, said that he would be with us always.

A fourth means by which God's purpose is carried out by his churches is prayer. This could be considered as simply part of the previous means. Yet, prayer is so important as a means to effective ministry that it ought to be given separate treatment. When Jesus came down from the mount of transfiguration, the disciples brought to him a boy who was convulsing and foaming at the mouth. Jesus healed the lad and was then asked by his disciples why they weren't able to minister successfully to him. His answer to them was, "This kind cannot come out by anything but prayer" (Mark 9:29). Here the Lord set forth the importance of prayer in the life of anyone who seeks to fulfill the purposes of God for his people. Clearly, we can do more than pray, but there is one sense in which we cannot do anything if we don't pray. Who among us would not admit that there have been times when we have sought to minister and have

failed to prepare ourselves through consistent prayer fellowship with
the Lord and through specific prayer with regard to the need that
we were seeking to meet? When such an attempt has been made
without adequate prayer preparation, one often experiences an awful
sense of powerlessness and futility. What a wonderful difference there
is when we move toward a particular opportunity of service with thorough prayer preparation and with a continuing prayer in our heart
that God will do his own work in the situation, empowering and
directing us during our involvement.

Prayer, then, is an essential means of accomplishing God's purpose
for his churches; but of equal significance as a means is the Bible,
with its message of redemption and hope. We do not employ it as
a magical talisman, like the African prophet who touches the Bible
to the head of a sick person in order to heal him but who never
opens the book to learn what it says. Yet we do hold that, for our
faith, it is the final authority, interpreted to us by God as Holy Spirit.
This is one reason why we keep the Scriptures at the center of our
proclamation and teaching. It is also one reason why we have such
problems with other groups (such as Jehovah's Witnesses, Mormons,
Christian Science, the Unification Church of Sun Myung Moon, and
Garner Ted Armstrong's Worldwide Church of God) who claim to
be Christian but who add other writings as sacred or set up a human
hierarchy or council to determine the "proper" interpretation of
Scripture. Another reason for our holding the Scriptures as central
is that the Holy Spirit blesses the sharing of them. There is a type
of self-authentication that these writings possess, even for many who
never saw a Bible before. In a number of places where Southern
Baptist missionaries work overseas, the approach has come to be that
of going into a village and asking the leader to read the Scriptures
(or have them read) daily to the people so that they may respond
as they deem fit. It is not at all uncommon for the national evangelist
or the missionary to return weeks later and find dozens of people
ready for baptism. In our own land, hundreds of essentially indifferent
Christians have come vitally alive through regular Bible study fellowships. Unbelievers who have been unimpressed by the personal opin-
ions and convictions of other persons have been captured by the
authority and simplicity of the gospel of Jesus Christ, as presented
by these same persons from the Bible. A final and clinching reason

for our using the Scriptures so consistently is the pattern of our Lord and the apostles, whose conversation and teaching continually mirrored their knowledge of and high regard for their Scriptures.

Another of the means for carrying out God's purpose for his churches is a suitable methodology. Some have objected to discussing methodology on the basis that they think we ought to follow the leadership of the Holy Spirit and not be concerned about methods. It is important that we seek the Lord's guidance as Holy Spirit in every aspect of our ministry, but this does not contradict the need of seeking guidance from him as to principles of methodology. Careful observation over a period of years makes it possible for us to discover methods which God seems to bless and others which seem not to be effective. A warning needs to be sounded, however, that no method should become sacrosanct and that the principles which we develop over a period of years must be adapted prayerfully and carefully in each given situation. We can also learn by observing the patterns of work in the life of the apostle Paul and others in the early church. In addition, we can read about the ministry of God's people through the history of the church. As we prayerfully examine all of these, God can help us in knowing what is the proper approach in the specific situation in which we are involved.

It seems that one of the great principles involved in so much of the work of God's people throughout history has been that of probing for response and establishing new congregations to serve as new bases for ministry and witness. The parable of the soils (Luke 8:5-15) indicates that the same seed sown in different places is going to bring different responses. If we discover that sowing in a certain place does nothing except waste the seed, it doesn't make sense for us just to broadcast the seed in a mindless fashion. This doesn't mean in the application of the principle that we should not share witness with people who are unresponsive. They need to hear the gospel and have the right to hear it. At the same time, in a very practical way, we should not continue to thrust the seed upon those who are totally closed to receiving it. What we must do is to stay in a ministering relationship to people like that and watch for openness at a later date.

This principle of probing would lead us to open many home Bible fellowships in our community, utilizing lay people in the leadership of each home fellowship. Through the months and weeks, as these groups are meeting, it will soon become apparent that some of them have a real vitality and ought to be especially cultivated. As they continue to grow and increase in their liveliness, some of them will develop to the point that they may want to begin having a full schedule of activities, such as those that are carried out in other congregations. When this time comes it will be necessary for the group, at some point, to seek the Lord's direction as to whether they should begin thinking about a kind of organized life with a separate meeting place or whether they ought to "seed out" and start one or more new home Bible fellowships at that time. In some cases it may well be that this group of believers will remain together, meeting in a home with a lay person as pastor. Such an arrangement would necessitate a program of theological education by extension in which such lay pastors would have opportunity for training and preparation for their responsibilities. Other home Bible fellowships will come to the place where they will feel that they want to combine with a number of others in the area and establish a congregation to meet together in a separate building, either one which they have built or a facility of some sort which they have rented.

The final means of accomplishing God's purpose for his churches is the one which really permeates all the others, and that is love. Regardless of how much a particular group of people may seek to serve their community and regardless of how much the individual members may seek to serve other individuals sacrificially, the element of love must be at the very heart if it is really to come through as a ministry of the Lord. Over and over again the Scriptures place love at the core of all that goes on in the Christian life. We are told, "Through love serve one another" (Gal. 5:13). Especially in the writings of John, love is a constant refrain; for example, 1 John 4:7, "Beloved, let us love one another, for love is from God; and every one who loves is born of God and knows God." In the gospel of John (ch. 15), Jesus commands us to love one another (v.17). In 1 Corinthians 13, Paul set forth the more excellent way as the way of love. Regardless of what else we may do or not do, love is the real benchmark of the Christian, for Jesus indicated that even the outsider would know that we were his disciples on the basis of our love for one another. Obviously, this does not mean that we can feel warm affection for everyone in the Christian community or outside of it. Rather, it means that as far as our own purposes are concerned we will desire and seek the best for those to whom we are related. And yet, when people submit themselves to Christ and experience his love together, there comes almost inevitably a warmth of fellowship, a tenderness, and a genuine affection which manifest themselves in a warm handclasp and perhaps a Christian embrace. But even more, there is the depth of commitment which rides over all circumstances and causes us to stay in relationship to that other person and to remain faithful and steady in our commitment to him. This is basic to the fulfilment of God's purpose through his churches.

In our consideration of the purpose of churches we have moved between two poles: God's glory (who he is) and God's love (his love for us and ours for him and others). Upon both of these poles, everything else must be focused; in these, all things find their ultimate meaning as made known through Jesus Christ our Lord.

4
The Types of Churches
DeLane M. Ryals

Do churches have differing personalities? Are there grounds in the Bible for beginning churches directed toward various segments of people? What are some of the factors in the New Testament which determine the type of church which comes into existence? Can we justify different types of churches in light of the biblical revelation?

DeLane M. Ryals is Director of Church Extension for the Metropolitan New York Baptist Association, New York, New York. A native of Oklahoma, he was graduated with a Bachelor of Arts degree in 1958 from Oklahoma Baptist University, and with a Bachelor of Divinity degree in 1962 from Southwestern Baptist Theological Seminary. He is a candidate for the Doctor of Ministry degree from Southeastern Baptist Theological Seminary.

He has served churches as pastor in Oklahoma, New York, Maryland, and New Jersey. He has written articles for Southern Baptist publications, including one for Volume III of the Encyclopedia of Southern Baptists.

The birth of a church is an exciting event. In preparation for such an event it is fair to ask, What *type* church is emerging? The type of emerging church tends to reflect the community in which it ministers. The people who make up its membership and leadership influence the type church it becomes. Even the meeting place helps shape the new congregation. Ministry emphases during the formative stage produce various types of churches. To the extent the church is an expression of the body of Christ, the Holy Spirit determines the type congregation that is born.

I've been in new churches almost all my life. As a newborn baby I was carried to the nursery of a new church in Oklahoma City where my parents were members. As a boy I made my faith commitment to the Lord Jesus Christ and was baptized into the fellowship of that young congregation. Sensing God's call to the ministry during my high school years, I began working as an assistant to the pastor of another new church that was being established on the growing edge of my hometown. During college and seminary days I served as a summer missionary, taking religious surveys in preparation for the establishing of new churches in the Chicago and Detroit metropolitan areas.

Virtually all my ministry has been with new churches. As a mission pastor on Long Island, I assisted new Bible study groups and chapels related to Farmingdale Baptist Church. Later I was organizing pastor for the chapels which became Towne Baptist Church in Joppa, Maryland, and West Monmouth Baptist Church in Freehold, New Jersey. My present work is with the new Southern Baptist congregations of Metropolitan New York Baptist Association.

Out of the study of these and other new churches I have reached some working premises in church planting:

1. *It is possible to celebrate both our uniqueness and our shared faith* as gifts of the Holy Spirit to the churches. Every church is unique, while sharing many common characteristics with all churches that belong to the Lord Jesus Christ.

2. *It is valid for a church to aim at target groups* of people in a particular geographical area. At the same time, no focus on the needs of one group of people is to imply a policy of exclusion of other people from a church. The target groups a church selects and reaches indicate the type church that is emerging. But if that church follows its Lord, it will demonstrate his kind of caring for all persons.

3. *It is necessary to organize various types of churches* in order to reach all kinds of people. Different people are attracted to different churches. Some churches are effective in reaching persons of a broad range of backgrounds and interests. Other churches tend to reach persons of the same culture. No one church can reach all the people. A variety of churches is needed to minister to everyone in the community.

To observe the various types of churches, let us look at the circumstances of the churches described in the New Testament and see how they resemble contemporary church situations. At first glance there would seem to be almost no resemblance between churches of the first- and twentieth-century worlds. Our world is complex and our church organizations reflect that complexity! Means of transportation and communications, to name just two of the variables, are drastically different today in comparison with the day in which Jesus walked and talked.

A closer look, however, reveals the similarities. Churches then as now are composed of people—human beings, forgiven sinners, believers. The various groupings, circumstances, preferences, and actions of people effect different kinds of churches.

Communities Require Various Types of Churches

"The civilization of New Testament times was urban," according to William Baird.[1] An urban community often requires a different style church than meets the needs of rural folk. Its agenda reflects its turf. Some urban communities need a rural-style church to minister to the needs of newcomer residents from the country. Some rural communities need a new style ministry to reach newcomers from the city.

1. The location is a factor in the kind of church that is needed. New Testament churches were established in metropolitan centers: Rome is estimated to have been an urban center of as many as one million inhabitants; Antioch of Syria and Tarsus may have had populations of 500,000.[2] Ephesus (population 300,000), Corinth, and Jerusalem were significant cities of the first-century world. There were even "suburbs" in the ancient world, including Daphne, near Antioch, and Cenchrea, site of a suburban church (Rom. 16:1) in Corinth's eastern seaport.[3] By implication, Acts 8:1 would indicate churches were established in towns and villages and possibly in rural areas.

There is a striking urban thrust in the initial missionary expansion recorded in the New Testament. It is clearly intentional rather than accidental that the missionary tours of the apostle Paul focus on the cities rather than the countryside. Such strategy cannot be dismissed as only the natural preference of a "city boy" like Paul. Peter and John seem also to have focused on planting churches in the cities. Cities represented concentrations of people and influence. The Holy Spirit was planting churches where the bulk of the people were and in those centers of most strategic influence over the surrounding territories.

Churches today may be classified by their geographical location. *Metropolitan churches* draw their constituencies from the entire metropolitan region. *Inner-city churches* minister to residents and transients at the core of the city. *City neighborhood churches* are made up of members from a particular neighborhood, former residents, or others who have family or friendship ties to that neighborhood. *Suburban churches* primarily involve residents of a particular suburb in their membership, though some churches reach into a broad number of suburbs. *Town churches* may minister to the town and surrounding countryside, as do *village churches*. *Open country churches* reach rural residents and, in some locations, residents of neighboring towns and villages.[4]

The church needs to define its geographical area. Even churches whose members travel great distances need to focus on ministry in "their own backyards." Churches minister to persons, not to real estate, but no church can afford to ignore its neighborhood or its immediate neighbors. The insensitive church becomes irrelevant to its world. Some churches need to redefine their geographical area to include the larger community. For example, a suburban church must accept its responsibility for sharing the Christian witness in its metropolitan area, including the inner city, where suburban members may earn their living. Linking lives and influence in fellowship with other churches heightens awareness of our shared responsibility.

2. *The nature of the community is a factor in the kind of church* that is needed. The cities of the New Testament were varied in nature. There were *government centers,* such as Rome, capital of the empire. Jerusalem and Ephesus were *religious centers,* meccas to their respective pilgrims. Some of the *trade centers* of the first-century world were Antioch of Syria, Corinth, Iconium, and Philippi. Thessalonica and Thyatira were *manufacturing centers. Military outposts* included Caesarea, Lystra, and Antioch of Pisidia. Athens and Tarsus were noted *university centers.* The first-century world included additional types of communities—port cities, entertainment centers, and cities with other distinctive traits.

Churches must be sensitive to the special needs of residents of their communities. There are unusual pressures in the lives of government workers, internationals, and multilingual residents of a cosmopolitan capital. Philippians 4:22 makes poignant reference to "those of Caesar's household," possibly implying there were government officials among the Christian believers in the church at Rome. The intense pressures on individual lives and the tremendous potential influence of the decision-makers point to the strategic urgency of planting churches in world capitals like Washington, New York, London, Paris, Moscow, Brasilia, Nairobi, Tokyo, and Peking.

The religious shrine city presents peculiar obstacles and unusual opportunities for the planting of churches. At once the "holy city" is comprised of deeply committed religious adherents and of spiritually receptive residents. New Testament Jerusalem is a case in point: The city could not have been much more Jewish in its commitment but that same Judaism formed the seedbed for the emerging Christian church. There should be a place in current church extension strategies for gathering fellowships of believers in modern Jerusalem and Mecca and Salt Lake City.

Certain cities are natural hubs of communications. Traveling sales personnel are continually radiating from the trade centers. At the same time others are transporting goods into the markets. It is vital that the good news of Jesus penetrate these centers, which in turn influence people over a wide area. That several New Testament epistles were circular letters (Colossians, Galatians, and others) is evidence of the strategic nature of certain key cities. Churches planted in Boston, Dallas, Los Angeles, and Anchorage have opportunity to make an impact far beyond their local communities through persons engaged in commerce and the communications media.

When Jesus spoke, the people enjoyed listening to him (Mark 12:37). That sounds like an everyday assortment of people—factory workers, clerks, gas station attendants. Mainstream Protestant churches are always in danger of moving upward socially and leaving behind the masses on the assembly lines of Detroit or Chicago or in the steel mills of Pittsburgh or Baltimore. New churches must be planted to minister where these people live. It should not go unnoticed by the churches that many trade unions schedule their regular meetings during our Sunday morning worship hour!

My limited experience as pastor to military-related families has shown me another strategic ministry: the opportunity to influence a broad spectrum of society through military personnel. Persons in military service often fall into one of two categories—they will either unite with a local church almost immediately upon arrival at a new assignment or they may never come in contact with the church. Many military personnel who do join the church participate in leadership roles during their tour of duty at the military installation. A great number of churches in Hawaii, Alaska, New England, and elsewhere would not have come into existence had it not been for the initiative of persons in military service. Military chaplains have served as pastors of some of these young churches.

There is a special kind of challenge in the university center. Paul confronted the intellectuals in Athens. Oxford, Princeton, Urbana, and Berkeley provide a similar challenge today. Vibrant, warm, spiritually alert churches in these communities can lead young scholars to "love the Lord your God . . . with all your mind" (Matt. 22:37.)

Through its membership every church has an immediate sphere of influence. For many churches that sphere of influence is its surrounding neighborhood. Some churches have specialized ministries to the financial community, the shopping centers, and business and professional groups in the places where their members work and live.

There appears to be a deliberate strategy of the Holy Spirit and the apostles to plant churches in key centers of influence, particularly in cities, from which the message would be broadcast over a wide territory. With the growing urbanization of our society, planting churches in cities is of crucial importance for the spread of the gospel to all of humankind.

The church needs to know its community.

Meeting Places Shape Various Types of Churches

In churches as in other organizations it is true that "We shape our buildings; thereafter our buildings [tend to] shape us." We popularly categorize churches by the buildings which they occupy: "She is pastor of that storefront church." "He's the preacher at the Tabernacle." "I'm the minister of First Church in the county seat." "*Where are you now?*"

New Testament churches met in a variety of places. In the Temple, in synagogues, in homes, in the open air, and in borrowed or rented rooms.

Our early American forebears had the right idea: "First Baptist Meeting House" or "First Baptist Church meets here." There was no confusing the congregation with its meeting place. But the physical surroundings do affect the life of the church.

The *Temple* is the first recorded instance of "shared facilities." It

was for a time the worship center for both the traditional Jews and
for the followers of Jesus.[5] Multiple congregations are needed in some
communities to minister to different language and cultural groups.
Sometimes these congregations can utilize the same buildings. The
mid-Manhattan ministry center of Metropolitan New York Baptist Association houses five fledgling congregations. English-speaking,
French, Mandarin Chinese, and Japanese chapels meet in different
rooms and at different hours on Sundays, while a Spanish-speaking
Bible study gathers on weeknights. The center serves as a launching
pad and first home for emerging churches in the city. Jerusalem's
Temple may also be the prototype for Old First Church or the cathe-
dral-type meeting place.

The *synagogue* represents the neighborhood church. Its function
sometimes resembles what Findley Edge idealizes as the church as
a miniature seminary for its membership.[6]

Homes ("Greet the church that is in their house," [Rom. 16:5; 1
Cor. 16:19; Col. 4:15]) and contemporary house-churches point to
the need for small groups for learning and ministry. A danger of
the house-church is that it may become so self-centered that it forgets
outreach or desires to remain "our little church." Home Bible study
groups are basic to gathering the membership nucleus in church planting today. Describing healthy, growing contemporary churches, Schaller writes, "There is an affirmative effort to function, not simply as
a congregation of individuals and families, but also as a congregation
of groups." [7]

The first-century church went public with *open-air services* on the
day of Pentecost (Acts 2.) By taking the message to the streets, the
church set a precedent expressing the validity of street meetings,
ministries where the people are, uninhibited by their fear of church
buildings or their suspicion of organized religion. From the day of
Lydia and her associates on the riverbank outside Philippi to the
stadium crusades of Billy Graham and the Times Square and Sunset
Strip ministries, there has always been an audience for the gospel
out-of-doors.

Borrowed and rented facilities have their counterpart in storefront or
"walk-in" churches of the inner city and in other temporary places
where young churches meet. This, too, has been an honorable tradition since the days of Acts 1. I have preached most of the sermons

of my ministry in nonchurch buildings—lodge halls, schools, motels, community centers.

Notice that these are interim meeting places for the church. Attractive, well-designed buildings can enhance the work and worship of the church. Most churches will eventually build or buy their own buildings. But the church is not limited to church buildings.

The church needs to secure adequate meeting places for its worship, training, and ministries.

Membership Influences Various Types of Churches

The church is made up of persons of varied religious and racial backgrounds. In the New Testament the church began with a nucleus of Jews and Jewish proselytes in Jerusalem. The next group to respond to the gospel were Hellenists, Jews who were influenced by the Greeks. Then came Samaritans, of mixed race and garbled religion. Finally, the church reached out to Gentiles: a black eunuch, who was physically ineligible for the established religion; God-fearing Romans (Cornelius and company), who adhered to the Jewish faith but were not circumcised; and to Greeks (in Antioch of Syria.)[8] The gospel quickly spread to centers of the Diaspora, where Jews and later Christians were in exile. I see parallels between church planting among the Dispersion and Southern Baptists in the North, East, and West. In both instances when the gospel was unhindered, it spread from the exiles to the local populace.

New Testament churches reached people of widely varying social and economic status. The Christian good news found response among slaves and working people and among business and professional people and even among high-ranking government officials. There is no indication of an arbitrary separation into class churches. To the contrary, the slaves and officials were in the same congregations. For instance, the Corinthian church included Jewish artisans (Aquila and Priscilla), a man of means (Crispus), converts from the Italian colonists (Titus Justus and Fortunatus), slaves, those able to travel (Chloe), and the city treasurer (Erastus).[9]

One segment of contemporary society deserves special attention in planning for new churches: the blue-collar or lower socioeconomic group. J. V. Thomas has documented the relatively high percentage of unchurched among the working class. He notes, "Most local congregations tend to be upwardly mobile . . . . If new congregations are not formed, there will be few opportunities for the working class person outside the church to 'get in' or find a church to which he can relate on his own socio-economic level."[10] Thomas advocates the establishing of thousands of small working-class congregations in the inner-city areas of our large metropolitan centers.

Before we too readily fragment the church into compatible groupings of "folk like us," we need to examine the New Testament pattern of a broad fellowship whose only unity is in Christ. This is not to say "the New Testament church" was perfect. It was not: witness, the church at Corinth. It may be inevitable that local congregations will develop as homogeneous units, but all these units are answerable to the Lord of the church as to their openness to all persons.

The New Testament world was multilingual. *Greek* was the universal language of the Mediterranean world, but people in various sections also spoke other languages. *Latin* was the official language of the Roman Empire, but seems not to have been spoken as widely as Greek. *Aramaic* was the native language of the eastern Mediterranean. *Hebrew* was the language of the Jewish Scriptures and worship services. The day of Pentecost accentuated the sounds of the *ethnos,* the peoples of the nations. The Diaspora had come home to Jerusalem for the feasts! It was in such a setting that the good news of Jesus began to bear fruit.

White, Anglo-Saxon Americans are regarded as peculiarly monolinguistic among the civilized peoples of our world. We need to heighten our sensitivity to the needs of persons who speak languages other than English. English-speaking churches must learn to communicate and minister to neighbors who speak other languages by forming ministries and congregations to reach them for Christ. Some churches need to become multilingual, like the French-speaking Baptist Church at Hanson Place in Brooklyn. Morning worship is in French. Evening service is in Creole, and the Haitian members feel more at home. English Sunday School is provided for children and youth, who are studying that language in school. Street rallies are trilingual, in English-French-Spanish to minister to the neighborhood. Every church needs to listen to its neighbors and find a way to speak their language.

Many churches will discover the practical expression of the hetero-

geneous nature of the church by participating in regional fellowships
and associations of churches.

Churches, as divine-human institutions, express the composite personality of the fellowship of believers, as well as the purpose of their
Founder. Each church has a distinct personality. Some churches will
be attractive to persons of certain backgrounds and expectations;
other churches will not seem appealing to those same persons. No
church has been successful in appealing to all the people. It seems
necessary to have a variety of churches to reach all the people. But
every church needs to be an expression of the spirit of Christ.

Forms of Ministry Produce Various Types of Churches

Every new church should develop goals to determine what type
church it intends to become. Some churches emphasize evangelism,
some ministry, some their educational program. All these are valid
emphases, having precedent in the Bible. Five Greek words typify
the life of the Jerusalem congregation that is reflected in Acts 2:41-
47. That was a worshiping people. *Latreia* represents the genuine
worship of God which changes lives, (Rom. 12:1). The people experienced *koinonia*, the fellowship of believers with their Lord and with
one another. The *kerygma*, the message of God's good news in Jesus
Christ, was proclaimed by sermon and by personal sharing of the
witness. The congregation engaged in *didache*, the teaching and training of one another in Christian discipleship. And they were a caring
people, fulfilling their *diakonia*, that ministry which reaches out to
others in Jesus' name.

Avery Dulles deals with these themes in his book, *Models of the
Church*. He describes five models. Each of them can be traced to New
Testament origins. Each of them has been in vogue at various times
in church history. Each has strengths and weaknesses.

The first model is "The Church as Institution." The institutional
model gives particular attention to official doctrines, rules for membership, and the structures of church offices.

The second model, "The Church as Mystical Communion," focuses
on the church as the body of Christ, emphasizing our fellowship with
God.

The third model, "The Church as Sacrament," expresses the idea of the grace of God made visible in the church to be a sign of hope in our world.

Model four, "The Church as Herald," is a more familiar Protestant concept. The church is witness and proclaimer of God's good news.

The last model, "The Church as Servant," points to "the urgency of making the Church contribute to the transformation of the secular life of man, and of impregnating human society as a whole with the values of the Kindgom of God." [11]

The church is more than an organization. It is an organism which derives its life from the Spirit of God. The church must fulfill its unique function of worship, but that worship is inextricably related to life. The church is a human community but also a divinely commissioned one. The church has good news to share, or we have no reason to exist. The church has a servant role, but ours is a particular quality of loving service in the name of Jesus.

The ideal is that every church would have all facets of its ministry in balance. The healthy church is maturing spiritually toward a balanced ministry to restore wholeness to persons and communities and our world. This, too, is church growth,

Religious denominations represent varying approaches to God. As H. Richard Niebuhr observes, "The division of the churches [into denominations] closely follows the division of men into the castes of national, racial, and economic groups." [12] By no means are the practices of all denominations, our own included, uniformly acceptable with God. It does make a difference what we believe and practice! But neither are all our respective traditions necessarily mutually exclusive. There is room in the family of God for every believer, whatever his race or personality or socioeconomic or denominational background. The Holy Spirit touches lives through a surprising variety of modes of worship. The ecumenical movement has not yet reckoned with the needs of various groups of people for varying forms of worship. Hence, different denominations are sometimes needed to reach the entire community for Christ. There is a sense in which the Southern Baptist Convention *is* an ecumenical movement, encompassing congregations of widely varying styles of worship and service.

A church that concentrates exclusively on public worship may wake up to discover it is a one-generation church, for outreach is a necessary dimension for growth.

A church that magnifies fellowship to the exclusion of all else may become a spiritual encounter group, mutually compatible but going nowhere.

A church that majors on proclamation of the Christian witness from both pulpit and pew has a lot going for it. But unless that church trains the new converts, its evangelism will only feed the cults and other religious groups.

A church that teaches and trains its members should realize stability within its ranks. It must put in practice what it studies or the church will lack dynamic.

A church that ministers to the needs of its community should never lack for opportunities. Such a church must constantly remind itself why it is ministering and discover ways to enunciate that "why" inwardly to its membership and outwardly to its community, as a parallel witness to its action.

Each emphasis is valid when exercised in a balanced perspective. What is needed is a worshiping, witnessing, ministering fellowship of believers who are equipping one another for continuous Christian growth and worldwide service.

The community, the facilities, and the membership interact as factors that produce churches of many different styles. But there is yet another human factor that influences the lives of churches.

Leaders Develop Various Types of Churches

The Bible introduces multiple images of church leadership.

Foremost, and most distinctive of the Christian faith, is the *laity*, the people of God. The church in the New Testament is composed of laity, both men and women, equal in the sight of God and active in the development of the emerging congregations. The theological term for their office is "the priesthood of believers" (1 Pet. 2:9). The church marked by strong lay leadership has exciting potential for growth and service. Properly understood, lay leadership should be no threat to mature pastoral leadership; rather it will enhance and multiply the work of the pastor. And lay leadership, rather than being stymied, should flourish in partnership with a pastor who is "equipping . . . the saints for the work of service, to the building up of the body of Christ" (Eph. 4:12).

I have observed the faithfulness of countless men and women who helped form the nucleus of emerging churches. Opening their own homes for meetings, these individuals have taught Bible study classes, visited in behalf of a new chapel, shared their faith on a one-to-one basis. They demonstrate the goodness of the good news of Jesus. It is out of such a corps that strong churches are born!

New Testament churches were often led by *apostles,* who became missionary church planters. The church has a continuing apostolic task—our mission to be agents of reconciliation between God and man. The planting of new churches today is one expression of our apostolic function. When churches, associations, and conventions link lives and influence in cooperative mission ventures, we are participating in the work we have been commissioned by our Lord to do.

The New Testament introduces the image of the *bishop* as a church leader. The title conveys the meaning of overseer, not in the sense of overlord but of administrator. (Notice that "minister" is at the heart of administration.) In first-century usage the bishop seemed to be related to a single congregation rather than to a larger judicatory. Wise church leadership is shared leadership. The goals most likely to be reached are shared goals which enjoy broad ownership by the entire congregation. Schaller asks, "Are the persons responsible for implementing the goals in ministry, service, outreach, program, and housekeeping responsibilities also involved in formulating these goals?" [13]

Building upon the Old Testament tradition of the prophets is the New Testament image of the *preacher-evangelist.* The image points to the message, the evangel, the gospel or good news. Some churches have declined for lack of good preaching; others have suffered when that was all they had! I believe faithful biblical preaching is a critical element in sustained church growth.

Early churches of Jewish background were strongly influenced by the *rabbi-teacher* image. The teaching function is closely related to the work of preaching in today's church. But the minister of a Christian congregation has broader responsibilities than are implied by the rabbinic tradition. We who follow Jesus need to recall his reputation as master teacher.

Another title Jesus applied to himself was, "I am the good shepherd" (John 10:11). The office of *pastor* conveys the shepherd image.

The pastoral role today carries a counseling motif. But the pastor must do much more than listen. A line from Milton continues to chide: "The hungry sheep look up, and are not fed." [14] The privileged relationships associated with the pastorate are not to be taken lightly. The pastor has the opportunity to lead the way toward a warm and caring congregation.

Henri J. M. Nouwen develops the image of the ministry of *The Wounded Healer,* one whose "service will not be perceived as authentic unless it comes from a heart wounded by the suffering about which he speaks." [15] From a more pragmatic stance, Robert H. Schuller states, "The secret of a growing church is so simple—find the hurt and heal it!" [16]

The most promising biblical image of the church leader is that of the *enabler-equipper* envisioned in Ephesians 4. There is a subtle but crucial difference between the people helping the pastor do his work and the pastor helping the people do their work. The New Testament opts for the latter: The pastor's office is to help the people of God do the work of the ministry. He is to be a leader among leaders.

Your image of the ministry and your self-image have a great deal to do with the effectiveness of the church you are leading. Schaller observes that it makes a critical difference in the growth of a church whether the minister adopts a "shepherd" or a "rancher" image. In young congregations a shepherd-style leader may unconsciously limit church membership growth to a manageable flock-size. He will develop the size congregation that one shepherd can tend personally, which may limit the church to two hundred members or less. The rancher, on the other hand, working with cowboys, foremen, and straw bosses, can lead the congregation in potentially limitless membership expansion. This kind of leadership develops churches which are clusters of many small groups.[17]

Leadership style profoundly influences the type church that emerges. The leadership factor must interface with the other factors of community, facilities, and membership. Some congregations respond to a collaborative leadership style. Others prefer more authoritarian styles. A few churches function best when there is no professional leadership. Some styles of leadership are needed at one stage in the development of a congregation, while different styles are required at other times in the life of the same church. Beginning churches need self-starter, self-directed, organizing pastors. When the congregation is better established it may seek a pastor-counselor or a strong leader in worship. Some pastors seem suited by personality and temperament to minister in the heart of the city. Other pastors, equally dedicated to the same Lord, may function best in open country areas. One pastor may minister most effectively in makeshift building arrangements; that same pastor could be out-of-pocket in a stained-glass setting.

The church needs creative, caring pastoral leadership.

Conclusion

The Holy Spirit determines the types of new churches. This should come as no surprise to us, for it is the Spirit of the Living God who brings the church into being. He gives gifts to the churches to edify the church (1 Cor. 14:12). Your brothers and sisters are God's gifts to you within the family of the church. Pastors and other church leaders are gifts from Christ to his church (Eph. 4:11). Treasure those gifts. Celebrate them! Use them by the power the Spirit produces within us and among us collectively. God brings us along as his cola-borers in the planting of churches. A new church is God's gift to the community. Through that fellowship God is working out his purpose in our world.

In a sense there is just one kind of church—the people of God, the Lord's church. But in a descriptive sense, there is an infinite variety of types of new churches, reflecting the beautiful diversity God built into his human family.

Every church is unique. Its setting is somehow distinct from all other communities. Its place, however humble or impressive, is special to those who meet with God and the rest of the family there. Its membership is entrusted with an unprecedented collection of gifts for ministry; and they can fulfill that ministry by their faithful steward-ship of their composite personality as a church. Its leadership will always carry its treasure "in earthen vessels" (2 Cor. 4:7), that is, in the strength and weaknesses of our humanity.

Yet all the churches have this in common: Every type of church is called to honor Jesus Christ as Lord!

Notes

1. William Baird, *The Corinthian Church—A Biblical Approach to Urban Culture* (New York: Abingdon Press, 1964), p. 18.

2. E. M. Blaiklock, *Cities of the New Testament* (Westwood, N. J.: Fleming H. Revell Co., 1965), pp. 86, 10, 19.

3. Baird, p. 24.

4. Ezra Earl Jones, *Strategies for New Churches* (New York: Harper & Row, 1976), pp. 36-44 for a discussion of types of churches very similar. See Lyle E. Schaller, *Hey, That's Our Church!* (Nashville: Abingdon, 1975), pp. 51-77, who discusses the ex-neighborhood and ex-rural church.

5. "The generation of Jews and Christians which followed the destruction of Jerusalem, not the generation which first heard the preaching of Christianity, is responsible for the completion of the separation [of synagogue and church]," James Parkes, *The Conflict of the Church and the Synagogue: A Study in the Origins of Antisemitism* (Cleveland: Meridian Books, 1961), p. 70.

6. Findley B. Edge, *The Greening of the Church* (Waco, Texas: Word Books, 1971).

7. Schaller, p. 150.

8. This analysis is based on an article by E. Luther Copeland, "Church Growth in Acts," *Missiology*, IV, 1, January 1976, pp. 13-26. For a fuller development of this theme see Frank Stagg, *The Book of Acts: The Early Struggle for an Unhindered Gospel* (Nashville: Broadman Press, 1955).

9. Baird, pp. 24-25.

10. J. V. Thomas, "The Church and the Working Class," unpublished paper, 1976, p. 16.

11. Avery Dulles, *Models of the Church* (Garden City, N. Y.: Doubleday & Co., Inc., 1974), p. 183. The five models are discussed throughout the book.

12. H. Richard Niebuhr, *The Social Sources of Denominationalism* (Cleveland: Meridian Books, 1929), p. 3.

13. Schaller, p. 152.

14. John Milton, "Lycidas," line 125.

15. Henri J. M. Nouwen, *The Wounded Healer: Ministry in Contemporary Society* (Garden City, N. Y.: Doubleday & Co., Inc., 1972), p. xiv.

16. Robert H. Schuller, *Your Church Has Real Possibilities* (Glendale, Calif.: S/L Publications, 1974), p. 4.

17. Lyle E. Schaller, "Looking at the Small Church: A Frame of Reference," *The Christian Ministry*, July 1977, p. 8.

5
The Beginning of Churches
Thomas E. Sykes

Why should we begin new congregations or churches? Does the Word of God support a church as it moves out in the planting of churches? Does the New Testament give Christians today some direction with regard to planning carefully to establish new congregations? Can we find practical matters which are consistent with scriptural principles so that planting new churches can be done more effectively?

Thomas E. Sykes is director of Church Extension and Brotherhood for the Arizona Southern Baptist Convention. A native of New York, he was graduated with a Bachelor of Arts degree in 1955 from Oklahoma Baptist University and with a Bachelor of Divinity Degree in 1960 from Southern Baptist Theological Seminary.

He has served as the pastor of churches in Indiana, South Dakota, and Arizona, as well as director of missions for associations in Indiana and Arizona.

Motivation to begin a new congregation may come from a variety of sources. The point of motivation may be the nudging of the Holy Spirit or perhaps the self-giving love of Jesus Christ, working through his people, to establish his church in a given location.

Look how clear the command is! The words of Jesus in the Great Commission spell out his total authority. (Matt. 28:19-20). He commanded the disciples to teach and baptize wherever they went. Mark simply reports the command: "Go into all the world and preach the gospel to all creation" (Mark 16:15). Luke's account is more detailed, (Luke 24:46-49). The fact that Jesus told his followers to disciple the world is the fundamental reason for the church to reproduce its ministry in new or unreached areas beyond its own specific location.

Jesus did not leave them to struggle with the task in their own weakness. He said, "But you shall receive power when the Holy Spirit has come upon you; and you shall be My witnesses both in Jerusalem, and in all Judea and Samaria, and even to the remotest part of the earth" (Acts 1:8). Old Testament prophets also received such a promise. Jeremiah is a good example. In his call to Jeremiah, God said, "Thou shalt go to all that I shall send thee, and whatsoever I command thee thou shalt speak" (Jer. 1:7, KJV). This kind of guidance promise continues to be a motivating force for God's people in carrying out his command.

The Spirit's guidance for starting new churches not only helped the disciples know where to go but also where not to go. Paul was forbidden to go to Asia and Bithynia (Acts 16:6-16). He was led through a vision to go to Macedonia and the city of Philippi. The word was preached. Hearts and homes were opened and the church at Philipi was born.

The implanted love of God in the heart of the church is perhaps the most compelling motivation for church extension. The moving testimony of Paul (2 Cor. 5:14-20) reveals the source of the mighty apostle's commitment to start churches. It is simply the love of Christ for a lost world. Thus he could say, "For me to live, is Christ" (Phil. 1:21). The purpose of Jesus became the ministry of Paul—so it should be in every generation.

Jesus declared, "The Son of Man did not come to be served, but to serve, and to give His life a ransom for many" (Matt. 20:28). He is the head of the church (Col. 1:18,24). The church as the body of Christ, is the "fleshing out" of the ministry of Christ, living and working in a local setting. As Christ gave himself for the redemption of man, so the church must be willing and ready to give itself in planned, intelligent, Spirit-led ministry. If the church is to be effective in this continuing ministry of Christ, it must be prepared to accept the role of his ministry. This includes his kind of motivation—love for a lost world. This is the love that brought Christ into the world (John 3:16). This love controlled and motivated Paul and the early church, causing them to establish churches which demonstrated and proclaimed Jesus Christ.

Our determination and success in church planting will be governed to a large degree by our motivation. We must examine our motives. The right motivation will ensure proper attitudes, consistent and dedi-

cated ministry, and patient understanding. Many new churches have
suffered early agonizing deaths because they were started with the
wrong motivation.

A church may well ask itself, What is our motive in beginning a
new church? Why should we be involved? A long list could be set
forth. Here are some motivating factors, though they might not be
said out loud:

—To look good among the brethren or make a good impression;
—Because people are lost and need to be saved;
—Pressure from the denomination;
—To solve an internal problem . . . get rid of the troublemakers;
—Dutiful obedience to Christ's command;
—The example of Jesus, Paul, or Peter.

Our motive for church planting may include some or all of these,
yet these in themselves seem not to be adequate. The most compelling
motivation is Jesus Christ himself, not just what he said.

The church is the body of Christ, indwelt by his Spirit. This means
that the church will be missionary, extending itself and reproducing
itself as it grows because Jesus himself is at work and about his Father's
business. He is doing what he came to do through his church (Matt.
16:18). The building of churches is his work. In the prayer of interces-
sion (John 17:18-23), Jesus indicated that he sent his followers out
in the same way he was sent out. He would send them to the same
world on the same business. This was reaffirmed as he spoke to the
disciples after his resurrection (John 20:21).

Our highest motivation for church extension and church planting
is Jesus and his compelling love. There can be no higher motive
for the church to be involved than to sense the indwelling Christ
impressing and continuing his ministry through us day by day.

Being moved by his love for our generation, it is natural that we
seek a strategy for a new work program that would help us avoid
pitfalls and maximize success. To have a strategy is to have a plan.
It is to have sound reasons for the decisions being made. The strategy
should be developed on the foundation of prayer and the guidance
of the Holy Spirit.

The strategy of church planting must include preaching and teaching that lifts up Christ as the way to everlasting life. This is the timeless
good news for every generation. This they preached and "those who

had received his word were baptized; and there were added that day
. . . souls" (Acts 2:41). The natural result of preaching Jesus is
decision. Those who believe desire to gather with other believers
for worship, prayer, and ministry. This is how the church began in
city after city. The Word was preached, people responded, and the
believers gathered in congregations for worship and spiritual growth.

It is natural for people to gather in homogeneous groups. These
homogeneous groups are identified as cultural and life-style groups
that include:

—persons differentiated by language, ethnic background or culture;
—persons differentiated by socioeconomic factors;
—persons holding diverse religious or cultic beliefs;
—persons limited by personal, physical, or emotional factors;
—persons whose "style of life" segregates them to a greater or
   lesser degree from the general population.

Knowing something about the characteristics of people in the areas
where a new work is planned is very important. Such understanding
helps determine leadership needs and the kind of approaches and
ministry most helpful. Effectiveness of the new work project will be
enhanced if proper consideration is given to the peculiar needs and
characteristics of the persons to whom we wish to minister.

To illustrate the importance of this, many urban-oriented people
do not understand rural illustrations. Many urban people desire more
formal worship. Because of cultural backgrounds, what is polite among
one group of people may be impolite among another. A person's
understanding of the Bible may be determined by cultural backgrounds. The leader needs to be able to relate to those to whom
he seeks to minister and to understand them. He should have an
appreciation for them as persons for whom Chirst died! He should
speak the language of the people.

Because he knew the backgrounds, Paul's presentation of the gospel
to the Jews at Thessalonica was quite different from his presentation
to the men of Athens (Acts 17). He used different approaches because
they were of different cultures with different customs. Their understanding of God and his relationship to man was very different. The
Greeks knew little of the Scriptures. The Hebrews did and recognized
it as the Word of God. Therefore, Paul had to adapt his approach
to meet the need of each group.

Frank Stagg indicates that the major purpose in Acts is to show the victory of Christianity:

> To show the expansion of a concept, the liberation of the gospel as it breaks through barriers that are religious, racial, and national . . . . At first we see only Jews embracing Christianity, and these thought that Christianity was for Jews only. One not born a Jew could enter the kingdom only by being inducted into Judaism. We next see Hellenistic Jews, Stephen and Philip, and proselytes active in the movement. Next, Samaritans, half-Jews, were received, though reluctantly by many. Finally, Gentiles were received, but this came by gradual steps.[1]

The apostles started where the people were. They spoke in languages their listeners understood. Knowing our field helps us to do likewise. This is an important factor in planning a strategy.

Another important factor is whether the community to be reached is permanent or transient in nature. Poor judgment is exhibited when thousands of dollars are invested in large buildings at a construction site where in a few months or years the bulk of the population will move. When this happens the few remaining permanent residents are burdened with an unbearable debt and the attendant problems. New work plans should be realistic and in keeping with the potential of the area to develop and support a continuing ministry. Options for worship places in transient communities are portable buildings, rented quarters, or mobile chapels.

In considering potential new work areas, we also need to take a serious look at the real need for a new evangelical congregation. To establish new work just to satisfy the ego or reach a preset goal for new work is poor motivation. It certainly could not be seen as New Testament church planting! New work should be started because it is needed and is essential to the fulfillment of the ministry and witness of Christ in a given area to a particular people.

The effectiveness and strength of other evangelical congregations in the area should be considered. Our new works should not compete with theirs but complement and add to the total witness of Christ in the area. Jesus reminded his disciples that they were not the only ones in his service! (Mark 9:38-41).

Closely related is a careful look at areas which are said to be saturated. This would mean that the area being considered has enough or even too many churches already. How can they be involved in church extension? Though considered to be saturated, a close examination usually reveals pockets of cultural or life-style groups that are not being reached by any existing church. These groups are usually open to the ministry of the gospel when it speaks to their needs.

Many of our inner cities or changing communities are in reality new communities. The buildings and institutions are the same. The people, the culture, and life-style may be different. This represents a new opportunity for new and challenging church extension activities. many such situations are in saturated areas.

Jesus and the disciples demonstrated that the gospel was for every person and every culture. They cut across social and cultural barriers to reach the rich and the poor. The good news was preached to the Samaritan woman, the Ethiopian eunuch, the Roman centurion, the Greeks in Athens, and the Jews in the synagogues. God's love for the world was demonstrated in the life-style of the early church.

Other opportunities for the church in the saturated area to be involved in church planting include cosponsorship of a new church in a more needy area. Where new work is often most needed, there is little opportunity for strong sponsorship support. With rising costs in property and living expenses, this kind of help can be invaluable. Short-term mission ministries to help start a new work or strengthen an existing work are also helpful. Assistance and encouragement should be given to laymen and preachers who feel called to go into new areas to help establish new work. A number of preachers not presently serving as pastors would welcome such an opportunity.

The vast resources of untapped preachers and laymen remind us of the parable of Jesus in Matthew 20:1-7. Some idle workers were asked why they were not working. Their reply was, "Because no one hired us" (v. 7). There is a need to provide appropriate opportunities for those who are available.

Responsiveness is a very important factor in church planting. It needs to be examined from two sides in relation to new work.

First, consider the responsiveness of the sponsoring church and leadership personnel. Where are we willing to go in the establishment of new church work? Anywhere? Everywhere? Are there areas where we are unwilling to minister?

Church extension may be in response to a need revealed by the

Spirit. Paul was the willing instrument to go to Macedonia (Acts 16:9-10). He sensed the need and felt God's call. For a church or a church leader to have such a clear call to a new work and to be happy to go is a delightful experience. A willing church and a leader with a sense of God's call will have a high degree of commitment. The new work and the sponsoring church alike will realize growth and joy as they share in the birth of a church.

One of my pastorates in Indiana responded to a definite need for a new congregation in a community forty miles away. A deep relationship developed between the mission chapel and the church. There was sharing of activities. A prayer partnership developed. A new excitement penetrated the sponsoring church as we shared with the Holy Spirit in nurturing the new work to maturity.

If a church is not willing or does not sense a need for a new work, it should not be pressed to sponsor new work. Forced sponsorship usually results in disaster. For lack of committed sponsorship, many missions struggle for survival. In the process, the mission pastor is often disillusioned or completely crushed by the experience.

Willingness sometimes is accompanied by reluctance. But because of a sense of call, trust, and commitment to Christ, the leadership moves into the new work opportunity with a faith that sacrifices personal feelings to the higher calling of God. Peter was willing to go to Cornelius with the gospel. Yet, his Jewish background made him reluctant. However, he did go after God showed him that he cared for and loved every person (Acts 10).

Because we are the body of Christ, we are motivated to go to those who are different from us. This may be the biggest challenge to new work a church may have to face. Are we willing, for Chirst's sake, to cross the cultural or life-style barriers to establish a new work?

The feelings and concerns for those to whom we go must be genuine. The motivation must be the Christ within or the efforts will be hollow, mechanical, and fruitless. The phony smokescreens of shallow interest or passing fancy will fade away in the midst of the difficult task of church planting. Remember Paul! He was controlled and motivated by the love of Christ (2 Cor. 5:14).

The other side of the coin of responsiveness is the people to whom we go. I met with a church missions committee about establishing a church in a new community nearby. The committee talked about surveying to see if a church were desired and needed for the benefit of those of our denomination. Clearly, there was an obvious need for an evangelical church in that area. They had to be led to see that work was needed in order to evangelize, not just to minister to our own. The purpose of planting a new church is to reach people who are unreached, as well as provide for those already reached.

We may not be invited to establish work in every place it is needed. Paul went in uninvited many times. Iconium is an example. In response to his preaching, a great many Jews and Greeks believed. The unbelieving Jews stirred up trouble. However, the disciples sort of "dug in" and worked all the harder (Acts 14:1-7). "They spent a long time there speaking boldly with reliance upon the Lord" (Acts 14:3). When opposition to the gospel came, they became more bold. The opposition also demonstrated the words of Jesus to his disciples in John 15:18-20. This kind of response to the gospel has often been repeated. Many believed. Many opposed. This is the dividing nature of the gospel. (Matt. 10:32-39). A new chapel being established in a small, rather isolated community in Arizona experienced opposition. There was opposition relative to the land purchase. There was opposition over a zoning problem relating to the placement of a portable chapel on the property. Services and a visitation program were begun. Considerable hostility was encountered from house to house. Some people said they would rather have anything there than a church. Work was slow and difficult, with little positive response. Soon a regular pastor was called who laid the groundwork for the new building. He encountered considerable opposition. The work struggled on, encouraged by a caring and praying sponsoring church. That pastor left and another came. At the height of the oppostion there was a threat to burn the new building if it were built. However, over a period of time, with determined firmness, Christian love in action, and the power of the Holy Spirit, a breakthrough came. The pastor was elected a president of the home owners' association in the community. God's love and redemptive plan had been felt through these committed leaders and the sponsoring church. Some in the community were reached for Christ. At this writing, the little chapel is soon to move into the building. The attendance for worship is in the thirties. They are located in the heart of a new and growing area. Hundreds of houses will surround them in a few years. The church will be there, alive and well, because a caring sponsoring church went where they were uninvited to share the good news.

Even in the midst of opposition, Paul and the disciples were determined to build a firm foundation. But when it became necessary to leave, they went to the next town and continued their ministry (Acts 14:6-7). There are times when we may be forced to leave an area of new work. Opposition should not be the only cause for withdrawal. Opposition, by itself, may not be a reason at all. There is, however, a reason to consider withdrawal in a new mission venture. That is when there is negative response from those to whom we go. Jesus could do no mighty works in his hometown (Mark 6:5). As he sent out the disciples, he instructed them to move on if their witness went unreceived (Matt. 10:14; Luke 9:5).

Paul had to move from the synagogue in Corinth because the response was negative. He went next door to the house of Titus Justus and continued to preach. Many believed and new work emerged (Acts 18:1-11). Eventually Paul and Barnabas turned to the Gentiles from the Jews because of their negative response (Acts 13:44-49).

Those who seek to plant new churches sometimes may need to withdraw from a specific location. This underscores the reason why we should study the new area carefully. "Probes" such as mission Vacation Bible Schools, Backyard Bible Clubs, home Bible study fellowships, or revival meetings help to determine the potential response. These activities help in making decisions for long-term leadership and financial investment. We should not waste time and money in chronically unproductive situations.

The Lord's leadership should be carefully sought if withdrawal is considered. We need not only the willingness to go anywhere but also the sensitivity to the Holy Spirit to know whether to continue or withdraw if the situation proves to be unresponsive.

New churches are no accident. They are born because they are caused to be born. The underlying cause will have a bearing on the strategy.

Some congregations experience what I call a "normal birth." The natural result of preaching the gospel is conversion. Many who hear will believe and be baptized. They naturally form into groups or congregations for further Bible study and worship. In the development of the early church, it was not only natural that believers in Christ gathered into congregations but it was also necessary. This was the conservation of the fruits of evangelism and the perpetuation of the ministry of Christ.

Jesus called upon individuals to follow him. This produced a group called disciples. He taught them and sent them out, expanding his ministry. This was the embryonic church (Matt. 4:18-25). The Lord continued to add to the group those who were saved (Acts 2:47). As the disciples spread across the land, they kept preaching as they went and new churches sprang up as the believers gathered together.

The results of evangelism continue to be a natural source of new churches. The evangelistic results may take place as a result of crusades, witnessing efforts, Vacation Bible Schools, Backyard Bible Clubs, Sunday Schools, and Bible classes.

Closely related to this is the emergence of a nucleus due to a growing sense of need in a community. An example of this is a new community where few, if any, churches exist. Christians in the area begin to talk and pray about the need for a church. They may ask a missionary or church to help them start a congregation. Following the first service in such a situation in central Arizona, I was told by an elderly couple that this was the answer to their prayers. They said, "We have prayed for a long time that we could have a church in our community." The church in that community was born and is growing toward maturity.

Migration of Christians also tends to bring about the natural birth of congregations. In the New Testament days, persecution scattered the church. Wherever they went, they proclaimed the gospel, and churches sprang up in their wake.

Our society is mobile. People in large numbers are moving to and fro for reasons of health, retirement, or profession. In addition, we have the exodus from the city to the suburbs and back. The changing communities which were left behind and the inner-city areas were mentioned earlier. Accompanying the return to the cities, are new high-rise apartments with their guarded entrances and the rebuilding of old neighborhoods. All of this adds up to a new life-style and new opportunities for meeting spiritual needs. As people move, concerned Christians contribute to the birth of new congregations which will be able to meet the needs of the influx of people in new or changing life-styles.

Still other churches are born as the results of purposeful planting. Sometimes the groundwork may be laid years before the congregation ever meets. This demands planning and a well thought-out strategy for church extension. Usually it rises from either the concern of a congregation or the determination of a single leader.

A congregation may, under the inspiration and guidance of their missions committee, foresee a need in a growing or neglected area. Seeking God's leadership, they make plans to meet the impending need. Accurate facts would be gathered about the area. Often land is purchased and set aside before prices rise as the development grows. When the right time comes, the sponsoring church sends out a corps of leadership personnel to help form the nucleus for the new work. This approach adds greatly to the financial and doctrinal stability of the new work.

The Creekwood Southern Baptist Church in Muncie, Indiana, which started in this way, began with a complete Sunday School leadership staff. The sponsoring church pastor, Lyndon Collings, and I visited eight of the most active and generous supporters of the church. We asked them to pray about being a part of the new work. Many did and a church was born. This new work had a solid start from the beginning.

The other side of purposeful planting involves a leader who has an area on his heart for a new work. Because he does, he visits, teaches, and preaches at that place. A pastor once presented such a challenge to me. He had an underchurched rural area on his heart. We worked together and conducted a two week Vacation Bible School. The second week of Vacation Bible School we had a revival at night. Around forty attended Vacation Bible School and over fifty came to the revival. Following the two weeks of meetings, visits were made, then a Sunday School and preaching program were begun. More than twenty persons were involved in that beginning. The pastor served both the new mission and his own church. Within a few years he began serving the new work full time. This is an example of a pastor who knew his field and had an open heart for new church development.

Paul worked this way. The Lord said, "He is a chosen instrument of Mine to bear My name before the Gentiles and kings and the sons of Israel" (Acts 9:15). Paul had a call to preach to those who had never heard. Some preachers have a call to new work, to establish new churches, or to preach to those who have not heard. Paul and Barnabas were called out by the Holy Spirit and sent by the church to this kind of ministry (Acts 13:1-3). God used Paul and Barnabas as well as others in planting new churches. The determined effort of missionaries and preachers responding to God's call to specific places is a valid and fruitful method of church planting. New Testament church planting starts with ministry, not the construction of buildings.

Unfortunately, some new churches are conflict born. They are born of the fruits of frustration—established as a result of feuding within an existing congregation.

The causes of these conflict situations are numerous.

Some of the more common problems are related to personalities, jealousy, money, relocation, building problems, or disagreements over methods and programs. Sometimes doctrinal problems or unstable pastoral leadership is involved. For troubled members, a new church may be seen as a means of escape. The leadership, however, may consider the new work a "surgical approach" designed to prevent an unholy war or rid the church of its troublemakers. Sadly, such experiences are often done in the name of the Lord. To say, "the Lord led," doesn't necessarily make it so! Work starting under such circumstances will carry the scars of battle for many years. In a neighborhood survey, I visited a home in which I was asked about the split which brought the church I pastored into existence. They spoke of it as if it had been yesterday. Actually, it happened twenty years before. We had no ministry to that home!

We need a more thoughtful approach to the problem of conflict in the church. If at all possible, the circumstances should not be allowed to degenerate to the point of starting new churches from the fruits of frustration. Churches experiencing serious problems should seek counsel from their associational director of missions, a sister church, or their denominational leadership. Many times such help can assist the church in finding a solution. If a split becomes inevitable, constructive planning should be done with the appropriate committees or persons. Every effort should be made to avoid a spiteful attitude. Careful consideration should be given to site planning and the relationship to other congregations in the association or larger denominational group. Applying the principles of sound strategy mentioned earlier would be helpful at this point. Every effort should be made to make the experience as constructive as possible. A reemphasis of motivation and ministering to the area of need could be very healing in such situations.

Consideration of strategy for new work would not be complete without a word about nurture. If it is important to give birth to a church, it is just as important to nurture and care for it as it grows toward maturity.

Paul's method included teaching the new churches (Acts 14:21-22; 15:36-41; 16:1-5). He returned often to strengthen them and check on their progress. The importance of providing sound and capable leadership for new congregations can hardly be overstated. Jesus also stressed the importance of instructing the new converts in the faith (Matt. 28:19-20).

Nurture includes the development of leadership, doctrinal studies, and stewardship of life and posessions. The application of the gospel to life is essential to growing effective new Christians and new churches.

Preparing the church for church planting is an essential ingredient of satisfaction and success. Preparation includes a committed and faithful missions committee. The missions committee might be said to be the "missions conscience" of the church. James Currin describes the missions committee as an "administrative service committee that makes studies, recommends plans, and administrates work assigned to it." [2]

Included on the missions committee should be the directors of the church's missions organizations such as Brotherhood and Woman's Missionary Union if they have them. Many brochures are available describing the work of the missions committee in detail. The committee is the working link between the sponsoring church and the new mission chapel.

A prepared church is also a willing church. It would be hard to say too much about the need for both the pastor and the church to be willing and interested in church planting. New work must be on the heart of the people if they are to succeed.

The pastor will be the key person in inspiring and instructing the church toward new work development. He cannot do it alone, but must have the support and encouragement of the people.

Some things can be done to awaken the spirit of concern for church planting, for example, personal exposure. Show the needs. Visit the site of spiritual need which cries out for a new church. A first-hand exposure to new work needs speaks louder than words. This will help to educate the church as to the needs of the community. Such things as potential growth, problems and problem areas, percentage of retired, youth, and working people should be known. Major interest areas such as industry, recreation, or retirement centers should also be known. Get acquainted in every possible way with the area of new work through

—prayer and messages. Specific prayer for guidance and concern is important. Bible exposition relating to the mission of the church and the growth of the early church grounds the new work in Scripture.

—testimonies of those who have been involved have great power of motivation and instruction. Such persons may be invited to share with the church their experiences in new mission work.

—personal renewal. The revitalization of commitment to God is involved in the motivation for new work. Books, conferences, and retreats for study and prayer can be helpful.

—training the leadership for their work in the new congregation is necessary for a good start. One who has been involved in church planting can be very helpful at this point. If such a person is available to help in the work itself, this also can be of great advantage.

The church preparing for parenthood should check and recheck its motivation and attitudes. Selfishness or desire for self-glory in a sponsoring church will hurt new mission work. Neither should the new congregation be seen as just a tool to fill the sponsoring church or help pay its bills. New work involves trust. We trust the Holy Spirit to lead, to save the unsaved, and to enable the new congregation to grow. We also learn to trust new leaders as they learn and grow. We trust the new congregation to grow in responsibility, make decisions, and assume an increasing leadership role in its own affairs. The new congregation should be encouraged to grow to be self-sustaining. Trust them to try. Overdependency can be crippling.

Steps to planting a new church have been set forth in a booklet, *Guide for Establishing New Churches and Missions.*[3] Jack Redford also has a book entitled *Planting New Churches*[4] which should be used by every church moving out to begin new churches. The church and leadership should secure these along with other material which will give practical guidance in the fundamentals of church planting.

Preparation of the church for planting new work should also include preparing to nurture the new congregation through its formative years to maturity. The task is not complete until the new congregation becomes a self-supporting, self-sustaining church. Happy is the young mission chapel who has a sponsor with the right motivation and commitment to see them grow to maturity.

With this kind of understanding the activities, programs, and plans are more likely to be what is best for the growth of a new work rather than just for the satisfaction of a sponsoring church. Knowing the burden of responsibility to come, the young congregation will more quickly take responsibility upon itself. They will find more meaning in stewardship growth and leadership development. The sponsoring church, too, will have the joy and satisfaction of seeing results from their labors.

Knowing when to constitute into an autonomous church is sometimes difficult. There are many elements to be considered, such as size, buildings built, and financial strength. Perhaps a sort of summary statement would say the chapel is ready when it has achieved doctrinal stability, a healthy concept of ministry, and the financial strength to enable it to carry out its God-given ministry.

Hopefully, when the new work is constituted, it would also look to a future of mission commitment and seek out an area of ministry and a place to plant another church.

Notes

1. See Frank Stagg, *The Book of Acts* (Nashville: Broadman Press, 1955), pp. 12-13.

2. James H. Currin, *Starting New Missions and Churches,* The Sunday School Board of the Southern Baptist Convention, Nashville, Tennessee, 1971, p. 11.

3. F. J. Redford, *Guide for Establishing New Churches and Missions,* Home Mission Board of the Southern Baptist Convention, Atlanta, Georgia, 1977, pp. 1-11.

4. F. J. Redford, *Planting New Churches* (Nashville: Broadman Press, 1978).

6
The Leadership of Churches
James H. Currin

Who are the leaders of the church in the New Testament? Is leadership a person or a function? What are the roles of leadership in the Scripture? Are all functions of leadership in the Scripture still applicable today? What are the responsibilities of the leader of a church?

James H. Currin is the executive director of the Baptist General Association of New England. A native of Tennessee, he was graduated with the Bachelor of Science degree in 1959 from Bethel College and the Master of Sacred Theology degree in 1971, then the Master of Ministry Degree in 1974, from the Christian Theological Seminary. He has served as pastor of churches in Illinois, Kentucky, and Indiana. He has also served as both state Sunday School director and state missions director for the State Convention of Baptists in Indiana. He has written leaflets, pamphlets, and articles for various outlets of Southern Baptist publications.

"Genuine living is not in doing what you like but like what you do." [1]

"The Lord redeemeth the soul of his servants: and none of them that trust in him shall be desolate" (Ps. 34:22, KJV).

New Testament Leaders

Even though leaders in Christian groups operated under a theocratic rule rather than a peer democracy, I found the following answers to the question, What is a leader? most interesting. James T. McCay suggests that "a man is a leader to the degree that: (1) he has a following, (2) his following is volunteer, (3) he demonstrates to people the best method of getting what they want, and, (4) he is the best man in the use of this method."

McCay suggests that people see a leader as a model. "His behavior shows them how to get what they want most . . . . They continue

to give loyalty to a leader so long as he keeps proving that he is
the superior man in the 'best method.' . . . . The needs of the led
determine the eligibility of the man for leadership." [2]

The primary thrust of this chapter will be an interpretation of Ephesians 4:11-13. Other Scripture verses referred to will be used in an
effort to interpret our primary text.

Apostles

The first title or office mentioned in this verse is that of "apostles."
In Greek the word signifies not only one who is sent but it also implies
that the person sent stands with the authority of the one who has
sent him. Apostles were men possessed by the spirit of God and
his will for their lives.

Little debate exists over the belief that Jesus appointed twelve apostles (Matt. 10:5-6). These men had been with Jesus and testified of
him and the power of his resurrection (Acts 1:21-22; 5:8; Luke 24:4,8).
There are suggestions, however, and some evidence that persons
other than the twelve bore the name *apostle.* It is obvious that Mathias
replaced Judas. Barnabas is so referred to in Acts 14:3-5 and Acts
14:14, and there's a suggestion of this in 1 Corinthians 9:5-6. Paul
and James, the Lord's brother, are also referred to as apostles. In
addition, some have used the names of Andronicus and Junias (Rom.
16:7). However, my studies of these brethren have not confirmed
to my satisfaction that they were ever apostles—but, rather, respected
by and closely associated with the apostles.

Tradition suggests that Barnabas was a member of the seventy,
rather than the twelve. These seventy were appointed and commissioned when Jesus was beginning his last journey toward Jerusalem
(Luke 10:1) and gave emphasis to the universality of the gospel. Ori-
gen contends that Andronicus and Junias also belonged to the seventy.

James and Paul are yet another matter. Paul defended his apostleship on two points: (1) he had seen Jesus on the Damascus Road (1
Cor. 9:1); (2) his apostleship had the Lord's own sanction (1 Cor.
9:2; 2 Cor. 2:12). The case of James' apostleship is not so authenti-
cated. Scripturel verses usually given as proof of James' apostleship
are 1 Corinthians 15:7 and Galatians 1:19. It is true that he was the
Lord's brother, and some hold that it was only natural that James,

who was also the leader of the church at Jerusalem, be counted among the apostles.

In all probability, James could have met the traditional criteria. An apostle must: (1) have seen Jesus and (2) have witnessed the resurrection and the risen Lord. Galatians 1:19, however, is in the accusative case—case of extension, whether in thought or verbal expression; Paul may well have used the word "apostle" here—an extension of thought and, subsequently, verbalization—to include James. It was also only natural that Jesus would have appeared to James, his brother, and, then, to all the apostles.

The authority of the apostles, while questioned by some, does not seem to have been limited to area or location. The apostles spoke with authority, regardless of place. They were honored leaders of their time and, along with the prophets, were the foundation stones of the church (Eph. 2:20). They also, with the prophets, were the original recipients of the revelation (Eph. 3:5). The function of the apostles does not appear to be administrative in the sense of a present-day bishop and should not be confused with such.

Francis W. Beare, in *The Interpreter's Bible*, points out that neither bishops nor elders are mentioned in the Ephesian letter, as an indication that we are still some distance removed from a developed organization. F. F. Bruce suggests that both the apostles and prophets of the first-century generation are the Lord's "foundation gifts" to the church. Lenski maintains that the apostles constitute Christ's gift to every single one of us, even to this day. We continue in the "apostles' doctrine" (Acts 2:42, KJV) as the foundation of the church and of our faith. Ralph P. Martin, in *The Broadman Bible Commentary*, Vol. 11, holds that those early leaders were witnesses to the incarnate and risen Lord and were vehicles through which he continued to express his mind to the church.

Donald McGavran believes that the first apostles spoke and acted from deep, personal conviction, not out of dogma or theory. Ronald Hill, who has done extensive study of *apostolos* and its attendant meanings, feels that Paul was an apostle and had a team of some thirty people who worked with him in establishing churches in many places. He further feels that this is the work of an apostle.

The duration of *apostolos* speaks to its function. A substantial number of believers today hold to the idea apostles and prophets still exist and function. It is true that persons may "continue in the apostles' doctrine" and, in some instances, function as did the apostles; however, it is difficult for me to believe that apostle, as an office, continues to exist today.

If *apostolos* continues as some claim, does this give those posessing such gifts the right of laying "new foundations" (Eph. 2:20)? Does it also give the right of new revelations as referred to in Ephesians 3:5? F. F. Bruce says that whether you interpret Ephesians 2:20 as the apostles and prophets being the foundation or as the apostles and prophets laying the foundations, either brings us to a one generation interpretation. Therefore, the foundation of the church is laid only once, with Christ as the cornerstone. Hence, apostles and prophets belong to the apostolic age only. By their very nature, it is difficult to see apostles and prophets belonging to a permanent structure of the church.

While William Barclay holds to the traditional qualifications for one claiming apostleship—that of having seen Jesus and witnessed his resurrection—he stresses that, in a greater sense, the qualifications are still with us. He means by this that a person who teaches Christ must know him and that he who brings this power of Christ to others must experience the risen power of Christ himself.

There are grave dangers, however, in attempting to extend an official office beyond its original intention or plan of God. Ours is a day of convenience and expediency and even some who wear the cloth may be guilty of using terms of titles for their own benefit and not that of building the body of Christ. Among those claiming to be Christians today are persons who insist upon titles and official designations. Some of those whose teachings are neither biblical nor Christian claim to be apostles. They also demand commensurate authority for the title they bear. This is open abuse of the Holy Scriptures and cannot be justified in the name of either scholarship or Christianity.

Prophets

The prophets were persons moving from place to place, declaring the Word of God. Some interpreters feel that Ephesians 4:11 refers to the Old Testament prophets. They do not believe that these men existed in the New Testament, maintaining that the "law and the prophets went until John." As J. D. Douglas suggests, however, early Christianity is basically prophetic. The pouring out of the Spirit of God upon all flesh does, indeed, carry with it the result that "they shall prophesy" (Acts 2:18). Paul (1 Cor. 14:1), admonishes the Corinthian Christians, "Desire earnestly spiritual gifts, but rather that ye may prophesy." There does seem to be a special group, even in the New Testament, known as prophets, and they were obviously set apart for the ministry of prophecy (1 Cor. 12:28-29; Eph. 4.11, Acts 13.1). Most of them were nameless servants of God who under the direct prompting of the Spirit (Acts 11:27 ff.; 13:1 ff.; 21:4; 1 Cor. 14:1 ff.) declared the "Word of the Lord."

They constituted the "foundation" of the church (Eph. 2:20), as well as being recipients of the revelation (Eph. 3:5). Foulkes asserts that the primary functions of the prophets listed were similar to the Old Testament. Prophets "forthtell" the Word of God. As a rule the prophets had no homes, no families, or any means of support. They, too, seem to have vanished quickly from the church. Barclay points out three reasons for this rapid disappearance: (1) during persecutions the prophets were the first to suffer; their occupation was dangerous, and they had little means of concealment—subsequently, they were the first to die for their faith; (2) as the local organization grew and developed, the prophets became a problem; churches soon had their own permanent ministers and their own local administrations; (3) while these prophetic wanderers had considerable prestige, some abused their office and lived comfortably at the expense of the congregations visited.

The *Didache, The Teachings of the Twelve Apostles,* which is the earliest book on church administration and dates back to just after A.D. 100, confirms both the prestige and suspicion of the prophets. Among those stipulations referring to the prophets were; (1) a wandering prophet might stay only one or two days with the congregation—and, if he wishes to stay three days, he is a false prophet; (2) if any wandering prophet in a moment of alleged inspiration demands money or a meal, he is a false prophet.[3]

It would seem improbable that anyone could read 1 John 4:1 ff. and Revelation 2:20 without recognizing that it had become necessary toward the end of that period to test the claims of prophets.

Evangelists

Gerhard Kittel, in speaking of the evangelist, says that "he is the one who proclaims the Glad Tidings." The evangelists continue the work of the apostles. "His task is to 'preach the Word;' be ready in season and out of season, rebuke, exhort, with great patience and instruction." [4]

The evangelists had neither the prestige and authority of the apostles nor the influence of the prophets. They well may have been the rank-and-file missionaries of the church who took the good news to a world which hadn't heard this wonderful story. They planted the gospel in various locations, and all of us are in their debt. Lenski holds it was their gift and ability that prompted them and not a fixed appointment, unless we are thinking about Paul's assistants. Evangelists are missionaries but they are not just missionaries, as suggested by Kittel, for "the term is congregational as well as missionary preaching . . . the gospel is not just a missionary proclamation (Gal. 1:5; 1 Cor. 15:1). It does not merely found the community; it also edifies it." [5]

These evangelists, for the most part, were nameless servants who shared the message of Christ with the world.

Pastor-Teachers

Some feel that when the writer of Ephesians used the phrase "pastors and teachers," he was two different officers which are joined together for the purpose of sharing the care of an established congregation. However, careful study reveals that the phrase "pastors and teachers" has reference primarily to the church leader—therefore, a single person. In multiple staff situations, these responsibilities may be divided among different persons without variation in the function. It may be that some pastor-teachers are stronger in one area than another. Some feel more comfortable in the area of shepherding or pastoral care, while others feel better while exhorting or teaching the Word.

Ralph P. Martin points out in *The Broadman Bible Commentary*, Vol. 11, on Ephesians that the one definite article in the Greek to cover both pastors and teachers is interesting and revealing. It suggests that there are two functions shared by the same individual, whose chief task is described in Acts 20:28.

Pastor-teachers were local, congregational leaders in charge of churches having been, for the most part, established or brought into existence by the preaching of the apostles and others. The responsibility of this early church leader was great, indeed. Truth was largely passed on by oral tradition and these leaders became the repositories of the gospel story. They were charged with keeping the great doctrines pure. This task alone must have been monumental when you consider the great throngs of people coming to Christianity from heathenism. They taught both the masses and the individuals. They served as shepherds of the congregation.

Pastor is Latin for "shepherd." Young Christians confusing the teachings of heathenism with those of Christianity were as present as the rising sun. The duty of the shepherd was that of keeping the flock safe. Acts 20:28 was a warning of Paul to the elders of Ephesus that they must guard the flock that God had committed to them. Peter exhorted the elders to feed the flock of God (1 Pet. 5:2). William Barclay deals beautifully with the experience:

> The picture of the shepherd is indelibly written on the New Testament. The shepherd was the man who cared for the flock and led the sheep into safe places. He was the man who sought the sheep when they wandered away and who brought them back again; he was the man who defended the sheep from their enemies and, if need be, died to save them.[6]

The shepherd of the flock of God is the man who bears God's people on his heart, who feeds them with truth, who seeks them when they stray away, and who defends them from all that would hurt or destroy their faith.

Early Leadership Changes

Leadership changes came early in the life of the church. The death of the apostles and prophets as official positions necessitated a change in leadership responsibilities. As the church was stabilized, the work of the pastor-teacher took on a greater significance. That official office, along with that of evangelist, still remains. As new converts began to congregationalize, the pastor-teacher became indispensable to continuity and stabilization. He both instructed the converts in the Word of God and served as a shepherd for the group. Even if the position is taken that apostles and prophets continued, direction sufficient for a permanent ministry could not have come from these men because this was never the nature of their role. This leadership came from one on location, listening to the day-by-day problems, and instructing people in the Word for the edification of the saints.

The gift of the pastor-teacher became uppermost in the life of the church. The basic needs of people have not changed. They still need to know God's will and plan for their own lives. They need to be taught, prayed for, and listened to. The shepherd's role of the minister can never be minimized. A recent survey stated that 42 percent of those who had sought professional help had gone first to a clergyman.[7]

Even in New Testament times, James, Timothy, and John seemed to hold a place of vast responsibility while serving as leaders of local congregations. James, as a model, would be followed in some churches as they grew and stabilized. Timothy and John also served well in this capacity. They met vital needs of the people as they served in the capacity of pastor-teacher.

These early churches were always on the edge of a storm; and Wendell Belew points out, "The church is a refuge for her people where they may find strength but, also, a battlefield where war is waged for the souls of man."[8] This type of situation was always in need of leadership, which was supplied by the pastor-teacher.

The evangelistic office, which identifies closely with our missionary situation, continued to exist and does so to this present day. The gift of the evangelist, along with that of the pastor-teacher, is required in each generation. Philip is an early example of an evangelist. He worked in Samaria and along the coast of Caesarea, sharing the gospel in new places. Kittel maintains that "all apostles were evangelists but not all evangelists were apostles."[9]

Wisdom seems to say that evangelists have continued to exist and to fulfill a vital function in the life of the church. They are both frontier and local.

The task of the evangelist emerged in greater prominence with the passing of the apostles and, as previously suggested, they became the successors to the apostles. The primary task of this group was that of declaring the facts of the gospel of Jesus Christ and that need will always be with us. J. D. Douglas suggests that from the Ephesians 4:11 message, "It is plain that the gift of the evangelist was a distinct gift within the congregation of the church and although all Christians doubtless performed this sacred task as opportunity was given to them, there were some who were permanently called and endowed by the Holy Spirit for this work." [10] With the passing of the prophets and apostles, the evangelists assumed greater responsibility.

Leadership Roles Today

In the church today, the pastor-teacher continues to be a primary leader. He is responsible to God, the congregation, and himself. As a professional, he must judge his own ministry. He cannot be carried away by the easy and generous platitudes of man, neither can he allow himself to be discouraged and disheartened when some inexperienced novice attempts to judge his performance. Each day of his life he walks before God, before his congregation, and before himself. He cannot do all the work, but he must see that all the work is done. If he attempts to do all the work, he will soon be unable to perform his primary task instructing, equipping, and shepherding the flock of God effectively.

The historical development of the church has brought with it administrative functions for the pastor. He is looked upon as the leader of the congregation and often held responsible for success or failure. It is unfortunate that churches today often use the same measuring device to judge a pastor's ministry as that used to judge a leader in the business or political world. It is equally unfortunate that some church leaders refuse any measurement or evaluation but prefer to hide behind ecclesiastical protectors to the exclusion of human encounter.

Brooks Faulkner has suggested in the book entitled, *Getting on Top of Your Work*, that some churches attempt to make a "god" out of their pastors. Some pastors enjoy this exalted position and allow their congregations to think of them in this capacity. Sooner or later, however, all will know that the pastor, too, is a man of clay feet—and when this is learned by the congregations who have deified their pastor to the exclusion of human reality the results are devastating.

A pastor must be concerned for the total well-being of the congregation which God has committed into his care. This does not mean that he can hold the hands of every parishioner every day of every week, but he can be interested and understanding. We live in a world of hurt and hate. If the gospel of Jesus Christ teaches anything, it teaches love. Pastors are models of that love. People learn to love through example. Pastors are church leaders on location where men's hearts are broken and bleeding. They may well be the only spiritual image some of these people know.

While administration in today's church has become necessary, a congregation cannot allow its pastor to become so overworked with details that he has neither the time nor the energy to perform his basic task of sharing and shepherding.

A church that expects its pastor to be a glorified secretary, a charismatic errand boy, and a dignified custodian forfeits its right to expect interesting and challenging sermons on Sunday. The most expensive secretary any church can have is its pastor. Too many God-called and well-prepared men have fallen into the trap of cutting stencils, getting out bulletins, writing letters, making trips to the book store, and delivering materials to members of the congregation. The real test of their ministry is whether they smile in the process. Any pastor who is preoccupied with this trivia has little time left for real study and soul preparation. Sermons are either "Saturday Night Specials" or warmed-over, worn-out sugar sticks that have lost their sweetness.

Churches need shepherding, but shepherding cannot be healthy without teaching. Leaders of today's churches must find time for spiritual and academic preparation. So much of the shepherd's work in the New Testament era was teaching that it became part of his title. The pastor's task is to equip fully the members of the congregation so that they themselves can minister adequately and intelligently.

The word *katartismon* which comes from the verb *katartizein* is an interesting word. The word is used in surgery for the setting of a broken limb or for putting joints back together. It is a bringing together of opposing factions. It is the mending of nets. It is putting a person in the place of service where he can serve effectively.

The pastor must, as Barclay suggests, see that "the members of the church are so educated, so helped, so guided, so cared for, so sought out when they go astray, that they become what they ought to be. The office-bearer of the church holds his office, not for his own honor but for the help he can give his fellow members within the church." [11]

The pastor or shepherd is often the peacemaker but never a troublemaker. He is a builder. He works to bring the members of the church into perfect unity as indicated in Ephesians 4:12. This is done by joint instruction and example. He is concerned with the maturity of the members, doing what he can to help them reach the full stature of manhood. They are to grow until Christ is reflected in their deeds, actions, and total life-style.

The pastor cannot contribute significantly to this beautiful and mature development removed from his basic task. He cannot obtain these results through merely human effort. This is a spiritual development and only a pastor who is informed by the Spirit can contribute to its function.

Donald McGavran has said that "the primary characteristic of the New Testament climate lay in its leaders. The apostles and missionaries were God's men, filled with God's spirit." [12]

As a church grows, staff positions become necessary for church development. Size, location, need, budget, and opportunity all help determine the number and kind of staff persons needed. Some churches have had excellent experience with part-time staff personnel. This has been especially effective in smaller churches. Employing persons even part-time gives specific responsibility to an individual for a certain phase of the ministry. It also places the work in a professional setting which has both advantages and disadvantages. This depends upon the attitude of both the church and the staff member.

Whether staff persons are employed on either a part-time or a full-time basis, care should be used in determining the job description. Some churches wish to "hire" someone to do the work. This is an erroneous concept. While staff persons teach by example, their primary task is, along with the pastor, that of equipping the saints to do the work of God. Neither a single individual nor a small group of professionals can do the work of a congregation.

F. F. Bruce's *Notes on Ephesians* quotes E. K. Simpson as saying, "In the theocracy of grace, there is, in fact, no laity." [13]

As churches grow larger in number, the need develops for a person or persons to direct certain areas of ministry within the church. One pastor can no longer give attention to the multiple needs of a large congregation. Some pastors have difficulty in assigning responsibility to others or relinquishing certain duties. Staff persons must understand their role and relationship, and so must the pastor. If the pastor-teacher is God's gift to the congregation for its growth and development, staff persons must recognize that they have been called to assist in that ministry. They should accept the pastor as the leader and understand that in the providence of God, they, too, are allowed to be a part of that ministry. They should always be supportive of the pastor and should never make decisions or perform tasks that would be detrimental to the pastoral leadership.

Staff persons must also be leaders. A leader never operates in a vacuum. He must communicate within the group he leads and they must respond to him. Effectiveness may be determined by the organization. Some groups have great expectations and well-defined plans. Others seem to have little or no direction—and if they arrived where they were going, they did not know where they were. A leader must find his way through the underbrush and emerge with direction.

Job descriptions will vary, depending upon the area of work assigned; but regardless of the area, the task of staff ministers is that of assisting the pastor in the equipping and development of the members to become ministers and perform their several ministries.

Lay leaders are in every congregation. They must be sought out, trained, and given responsibility commensurate with their talents and experience. A church that hires a staff of professionals to do the work of the ministry is likely to ignore some of God's choicest servants. This is not to suggest professionals should not be employed—but to emphasize again the danger of professionals monopolizing the church's ministry. Someone has said, "Greater is he that multiplieth the doers than he that doeth."

Lyle Schaller refers to church leaders as "enablers," helping people carry out their ministry.

Think for a moment of the vast, untapped reservoir of capable, talented, dedicated lay persons in the churches. Many of them are sitting idle because "no one has hired them." They do not expect monetary remuneration. Their reward for service is that which money cannot buy. Think, again, what these lay leaders could mean in enlisting and equipping other lay persons. Think of what Southern Baptists could do in this day of Bold Mission Thrust if thousands of lay persons, presently not involved, began to minister. This will happen best when they are "fully equipped" and have fully matured.

Until then, we must keep on recruiting, instructing, and developing lay leaders. A paid professional staff has no greater function. This is the greatest potential of our churches today.

Many lay leaders can be enlisted by following a rather simple suggestion. Ask these persons to serve in an area of their interest and/or expertise. They are busy people and often feel that they do not have the time to retrain or learn again how to do a work in a different area or different age group. "Ring their bell—push their button" by talking to them about positions interesting to them.

Some lay persons, particularly those of the executive and professional ranks, will respond to short-term commitments. That is a beginning point; do not underestimate its value. Regardless of the procedure, we must have thousands of lay leaders responding to the ministries of the church if we are going to meet the challengers of this day. Once they have been enlisted, do not forget to keep the doors of communication open.

Leadership Responsibilities

The leaders of the church have an awesome responsibility. They must see that a church is involved in Christ's work. The needs of any generation do not permit the luxury of indifference, ineffectiveness, or idleness.

The gospel of Jesus Christ is the hope of this world and that gospel must be shared with all. The church can never be contented that her people are merely decent and respectable, but they must be on mission for Jesus Christ if his command is to be fulfilled. The pastor, the staff, and lay leaders must be commonly concerned that people are doing his work. They are his army and, to be effective, must march at his command.

Christians within a church are so uniquely bound together that it is impossible for one member to be all that he can be without the other members being what they should be. Church members, both from within the ranks of those professionally trained and those from within the membership, must understand this concept if a church is to accomplish its task in the world. Otherwise, it will speak its message in isolation and not in relation to the world to whom it is sent. The message it proclaims will fall on deaf ears. Too many churches have destroyed their effectiveness by their lack of unity.

A church must proclaim the message of Jesus Christ. It must evangelize and teach. It cannot ignore the admonition to equip the saints and to build the congregation both spiritually and numerically. It needs to disciple those it reaches and contribute to the maturing of both the individual and the masses. Its program must speak to this ministry. This unity and these functions are a priority. Leaders are responsible for these actions. A church, regardless of name, prestige, or any other factor, can never be what God intended without them.

The value of this type of fellowship may best be described by a letter that came to my desk just as I was finishing the manuscript for this chapter. It is shared exactly as received:

> Dear Jim,
> I just thought I would express my thanks and appreciation again for the love and friendship that you and others at Northside have shown toward my family and me. We had no idea that church and living for the Lord would be so much fun.
> I have attended churches that were very impersonal and cold but this just isn't the case at our church.
> Thanks again to both yourself and Margie for coming by that night and helping us make the decision that we had wanted to make for a long time.
>
> God Bless You!
> Dave

Leaders must lead. What kind of leader are you? I pray that these words may help us all rediscover the significance of our role as leaders. If so, churches will advance; and all of us will reap the reward that comes from being as well as doing.

Notes

1. Roy O. McClain, *If with All Your Heart* (Westwood: Fleming H. Revell Co., 1961), p. 101.

2. James T. McCay, *The Management of Time* (Englewood, N. J.: Prentice-Hall, Inc., 1959), pp. 5, 6.

3. William Barclay, *The Letters to the Galatians and Ephesians* (Philadelphia: Westminster Press, 1958), p. 173.

4. Gerhard Kittel, ed., *Theological Dictionary of the New Testament* (Grand Rapids: Eerdmans Publishing Co., 1973), p. 737.

5. Ibid., pp. 737, 734.

6. Barclay, p. 175.

7. *Americans View Their Mental Health*, p. 307.

8. M. Wendell Belew, *Churches and How They Grow* (Nashville: Broadman Press, 1971), p. 20.

9. Kittel, p. 737.

10. J. D. Douglas, *The New Bible Dictionary* (Grand Rapids: Eerdman's Publishing Co., 1973), p. 400.

11. Barclay, p. 176.

12. Donald McGavran, *Church Growth and Christian Mission* (New York: Harper & Row, 1965), p. 28.

13. F. F. Bruce, *The Epistle to the Ephesians* (Westwood: Fleming H. Revell, Co., 1968), p. 86.

7

The Relationship of Churches

Hugh O. Chambliss

Are churches absolutely and totally independent or isolated from other churches? How were the churches of the New Testament related to each other? Is there in Scripture a unifying principle for churches to work together? What are the various bodies of organizational structure to which Southern Baptist churches are related? Can Southern Baptist churches live isolated completely from non-Baptist churches and parachurch organizations? What are the values to be found as churches are related together? How can a local church maintain its relationship with other churches with which it chooses to work?

Hugh O. Chambliss is the executive director of the Madison Baptist Association, Huntsville, Alabama. A native of Alabama, he was graduated from Howard College (now Samford University) and with a Master of Divinity degree in 1951, from the Southern Baptist Theological Seminary. He received a Doctor of Divinity degree in 1974 from Samford University.

He has served as the pastor of churches in Alabama and Kentucky, as well as director of missions previously. He has written articles for several Convention periodicals.

Introduction

When any group of Christians get together with the idea of beginning or planting a new church, they must of necessity consider the relationships that church will have after its beginning. The constituting of a Christian church should never be considered to be a private matter.

When Paul wrote to the Christians in Corinth that "we are God's fellow-workers" (2 Cor 3:9), he not only set out a principle that had to do with one Christian's relationship to God through Christ but also the relationship of one Christian to another Christian and the relationship of one church to others.

When Jesus used the term *ekklesia* to identify his followers in Matthew 16, he strongly implied they were to have many unique relationships as did the town meeting groups of Bible times which were also *ekklesias*. The very nature of the Christian life makes Christian group relationships natural and normal.

The purpose of this chapter will be to consider the relationships of churches to churches.

Church Relationships in Acts

One does not need to read very far in the book of Acts to see that the early Christians were not only bound together in congregations but also bound together in groups of congregations. When Philip went from Jerusalem to preach in Samaria (Acts 8:5 ff.) and some people were converted, he needed help to disciple them. The church at Jerusalem heard of his work and sent Peter and John to give Philip support and to assist the young Christians. This was a very natural, normal, and gracious thing for the Jerusalem church to do. It was mutually desired, fully acceptable, and very helpful to both groups of Christians. A meaningful fellowship was easily established between these two groups.

A similar thing took place between the Jerusalem church and the Antioch church (Acts 11:19 ff.). The Antioch church was exploding with growth. They needed a hand from someone else. The church at Jerusalem dispatched Barnabas to Antioch to assist the church. He not only personally encouraged the believers but he also went to Tarsus and invited Paul to come and help out. As a result of this natural experience, these two churches established a beautiful, meaningful, and lasting relationship around which the early churches were later to build and develop strong and meaningful church fellowships.

When the Antioch church was struggling with the problem of whether circumcision was a prerequisite to salvation and church membership, the Antioch congregation sent Paul, Barnabas, and a small committee to get counsel from the older and stronger Jerusalem church (Acts 15). This meeting which became known as the Jerusalem Council helped this church out of its grave problem and became extremely significant in shaping the destiny of the Christian movement from then on.

When the churches in Asia Minor were struggling with this and other problems, the Antioch church, no doubt remembering the assistance of the Jerusalem church, encouraged Paul and his associates to go to their aid and to share the ideas which they and the Jerusalem church had agreed upon with the Asian churches (Acts 15:40; 16:4).

Throughout the entire book of Acts, this relational spirit of Christianity is evident. When carefully observed, it can be a beautiful experience of Christians and groups of Christians or Christian churches relating dynamically to each other.

Factors in the Fellowships

As churches today look to the spirit and practice of the early New Testament churches, several things stand out for consideration in establishing relationships.

The early churches developed deep and meaningful fellowships through their gatherings. By getting together they came to know and to love each other. They developed a spirit of friendship and fellowship in Christ which bound them together, sustained, and strengthened them in their personal lives, their homes, and the ministry of their churches.

These fellowshipping churches also developed valid theological and doctrinal unity through their councils. The faith developed by these young churches was solid, strong, and vigorous enough to not only meet their own personal needs but to also withstand the assaults of pagan religions with which they were confronted and to stand the test of time for use by Christians today. No one church or person accomplished this alone. While Paul certainly articulated the great doctrines more than any other person, these doctrines were not his alone. While the Jerusalem and Antioch churches were significant churches in the unifying of "the faith," it was not theirs alone. The vital doctrines and theological concepts of the New Testament Scriptures were experienced and wrought out by God as he led in the day-by-day experiences of all the New Testament churches. This is not to say the councils and get-togethers were not crucial to the finished doctrinal concepts of the New Testament churches. They were. However, the councils only reflected the outworking of the experience through which the early churches were being led. Without the relationships experienced by those early churches, we would not have the "unity" of doctrine we find in the Bible today.

Furthermore, through association with each other the churches of the New Testament set an example and cut a pattern of Christian ministry that was based on love, care, and concern.

The early churches seemed to feel they could never do enough to help each other as well as to assist unbelievers. Perhaps more than reciprocal love, their love was the *agape* kind of love about which Christ spoke and demonstrated. The church at Antioch decided "in the proportion that any of the disciples had means, each of them determined to send a contribution for the relief of the brethren living in Judea" (Acts 11:29). Paul doesn't forget to write in his second letter to the Corinthians how the churches in Macedonia were so moved by their love for Christ, that "according to their ability, and beyond their ability they gave" for Paul to share with the needy Christians in the church at Jerusalem (2 Cor. 8:3).

The early churches also demonstrated the value of open communication so necessary to good relationships. While they had problems, they did not let those problems isolate them from each other. They stayed on speaking terms while working out the problems within their own churches and between each other. After the Jerusalem Conference (Acts 15), the church at Jerusalem not only sent two representatives to communicate their feeling to Antioch and the other churches but they also sent a letter that clearly and cordially set out their thinking (Acts 15:23-29). The early churches also prayed for each other. When the church at Antioch commissioned Paul and Barnabas as missionaries, "they prayed . . . and sent them away" (Acts 13:3). Afterwards, as they were going again, they went "being committed by the brethren to the grace of the Lord" (Acts 15:40) to encourage the churches.

In Ephesians Paul reminded the church at Ephesus to "be on the alert with all perserverance and petition for all the saints" (6:18). Through prayer, they supported and undergirded each other and were more closely bound together by doing so.

The early churches also developed simple but orderly systems, organizations, and structures that made it possible for them to function effectively together. Examples of this are the Jerusalem Conference (Acts 15); the commissioning of Paul and Barnabas (Acts 13); the plan for aiding each other (Acts 11:29 and 2 Cor. 8:1); Paul and

Silas reporting to the churches at Antioch (Acts 15:27) and Jerusalem (Acts 21:18-19). These examples indicate the outgrowth and development of an orderly, functional system that advanced as the number of churches grew, the churches moved farther out into the world, and the ministry of the church was expanded. These serve as valid justification of plans and systems for expediting the work of the churches today.

Free Churches Functioning Together

The precedent of churches functioning together is well-established in the New Testament and is very valid for churches today. The relational spirit of the New Testament churches may be best described as one in which they saw themselves as free churches under Christ, functioning together.

They apparently never really thought of themselves as independent churches. They seem to have felt very dependent upon God, upon the Holy Spirit, and upon each other. The idea of the church in the New Testament in relationship to other churches is the idea of freedom, not independence. This concept is not a play on words or a matter of semantics but rather involves a dynamic principle. To be free, one does not have to be independent. Freedom always begets initiative, freedom provides opportunity, and freedom demands responsibility. Freedom is more than independence. It is better than independence. At the same time relational independence implies isolation and self-sufficiency. These are not scriptural ideas of a church, neither are they compatible with the nature and purpose of "the church" or the spirit of Christ. New Testament churches were not independent churches. They were free churches but they functioned together.

Through the years connectional systems of churches and attitudes toward them have varied much as they do today. Systems have ranged from the concept of complete independence and isolation of some churches to the concept of the Roman Catholic Church with its absolute papal authority. Perhaps it is between the two extremes that the New Testament pattern of church relationships may be found.

For organizations of churches to become more than that of free churches functioning together may be for them to be involved in ecclesiastical systems for which there is no New Testament example.

On the other hand for churches to fail to have some sort of meaningful relationship with other churches may be for them to remove themselves from the New Testament pattern, in which case they would assume an independence that the New Testament churches never practiced. An absolute separatist idea for a church is unscriptural. The independent, separatist attitude fragments the church and does violence to the cooperative spirit found among the New Testament churches. Absolute ecclesiastical authority in relational Christianity goes beyond the example of the New Testament. In between the extremes is the ideal. The New Testament ideal may be best seen simply as a dynamic fellowship of free churches functioning together.

The Relational Structures of Baptists

Nearly all churches of every "faith" today have some formal or informal relationship with other churches. These range from the absolute authoritarian concept of some church systems to small parachurch groups who do not claim to be churches but in essence function as churches and even as denominations of churches. In between, are the churches who function in the organized framework of conventions, conferences, and associations. Even those churches claiming to be independent nearly always have some ties with other churches through which they function in one way or another. A newspaper announcement in an Alabama city carried the note that "The North Alabama Fellowship of Independent Baptist Churches will meet and elect officers."

Southern Baptist churches have through the years normally and naturally organized themselves into three distinct functional units of life and work through which they live and work together. Each of these came into existence because it was recognized by the churches that they were needed to get the work of Christ done as they felt they were supposed to do it. Their motivation was probably both spiritual and practical. The Southern Baptist units of organization are the county or district associations, the state or regional conventions, and the Southern Baptist Convention, which is national in scope. The Baptist World Alliance is a world fellowship of Baptists through which conventions and unions of Baptists do some work together but is mostly for fellowship.

Affiliation with each of these organizations is entirely voluntary and optional for the church. Acceptance is also optional for the units of organization with which the church may desire affiliation.

Each one of these units of organization is vitally important to the total functional process of the churches related to them. In relative terms, one is no more important than the other. Each has its specific purpose for being and its own sphere of usefulness in the overall functioning process of a church. Affiliations of churches in these structures are not strictures but are actually liberating forces. These organizations help provide ways and means for the church to do what it wishes to do as a church. A church is truly free only when it has a way to do what it wants and needs to do. Otherwise it is confined. These units are most effective when each functions in its own basic sphere of purpose.

Through their associations some of the work of Baptists is done best. Through the state conventions other things are done better. Through the Southern Baptist Convention some things may be done that cannot be done through either the association or state conventions. These units of organization are in reality the churches extending themselves beyond themselves. Because of this it is imperative that leaders of each unit of organization, as well as the churches, know and understand their specific purpose and their place in the overall functional process. A relational system, such as Baptists have, functions best when the structure is maintained in low profile, with the churches having the greater visability. Such a structure requires that leadership be strong and able but not domineering in its attitude. Whenever churches see these units of organization as their means of fulfilling their divine purpose, affiliation with them and work through them becomes more exciting, worthwhile, and enjoyable.

The Establishing of Affiliations

The means of a church being formally related to other churches varies from one church group to another. In some bodies the local congregation has no choice. In the Roman Catholic concept of "The Church," every local congregation is unquestionably governed by the Catholic Church as a whole, through its hierarchy. To a lesser degree some groups such as Methodists, Episcopalians, Presbyterians, and others have authoritative ecclesiastical systems. Among Baptists, each church or congregation itself decides if it is to be affiliated with other churches in any or all of the Baptist units, as well as to what degree it will "associate" or "cooperate" with any other non-Baptist group.

The two most frequent ways Baptist churches are begun are through an already organized, established church sponsoring a mission church or chapel or by a group of people getting together to start on their own without any sponsorship. From a practical standpoint a young church nearly always needs the care and concern of an older and stronger church. The sponsorship of an organized church can always be helpful to a new congregation. If a new church or chapel is sponsored by an organized church, great care is taken to see that the new congregation grows and develops into a well-organized, effectively functioning church. Both the sponsoring church and mission will recognize and respect their relationships to each other. They will carefully determine in the beginning what these relationships are and see that they are faithfully maintained. Some matters they must determine are the calling of a pastor, the election of leadership, control of finances, ownership of property, time of formal organization, and beginning of self-government. While flexibility is crucial to the maintenance of all good relationships, hasty and arbitrary action by a mission or its sponsoring church can do great harm to both. Mutual responsibility and trust by church and mission are very important to both.

Quite often, churches begin out of dissension and do not desire any relationship to another church. Obviously this can produce an unwholesome attitude.

Formal affiliation of Baptist churches is initiated by the congregation itself, whether it be a sponsored or unsponsored mission, church, or chapel. Affiliations of churches in the state convention and Southern Baptist Convention are usually less formal than affiliation in an association.

The affiliation of a church with other churches in a Baptist association is usually the point at which a new congregation's affiliation with all units of organized Baptist life is initially decided. It would be a rare thing for a church to become affiliated with a state convention or the Southern Baptist Convention before it did with an association. In a few cases, a church once affiliated with an association but no longer actually "related" to the association, continues to participate in state conventions and Southern Baptist Convention life. This is not the rule, but the exception. The fact that this is true however, probably points up a distinction between the district associations and the state conventions. In a church's affiliation with other churches in an association both "faith and practice" are extremely crucial, while in the larger relationship, where churches are not as well known to each other, shades of theology and doctrine become less significant and practice and presence tend to take precedence over doctrine. However, churches differing significantly in doctrine or philosophy will ordinarily soon decide themselves that they do not wish to continue affiliation even in the larger groups and formally or informally withdraw.

To establish formal relationships with a Baptist association, a church "petitions" or "requests" acceptance by that group. Whether called membership, as is the case with some associations, or affiliation, as it is called by others, makes little difference. Mutual acceptance on the part of the petitioning church and associated churches has proven to be of more significance than the terminology of constitutions. A church having no intention of really being actively associated with other churches of an association or convention should never offer itself for affiliation with the other churches. Lack of basic compatibility can only lead to frustration and unhappiness for the church and mean little or nothing to the other churches with whom it may be nominally affiliated.

The procedure followed in the affiliation process is ordinarily rather simple. The congregation first decides to request "affiliation" with an association. It presents its request to the credentials or affiliations committee of the association. The credentials committee determines whether to recommend the church for affiliation based on the criteria the association has set out in its constitution. If approved by the credentials committee, the church will be presented to the formal meeting of the association for the approval or rejection. In some cases a period of time for "watchcare" is required for final action, usually a year. In other cases affiliation is approved immediately and messengers from the churches are welcomed as part of the fellowship of that association. Churches affiliate through associations and conventions. Messengers from the affiliated churches make up the functioning body of associations and conventions and are also autonomous, having no authority over the churches from which they come. Ordinarily a part of the consideration of an association for a church to be affiliated with it is whether the petitioning church is participating in the life and work of the state and national conventions, as well as the work of the association.

Churches rarely desire to be a part of an association if they do not wish to also participate in the fellowship and work of the conventions. It is primarily through the Convention that they do their literature publishing, college and seminary training, annuity programs, and do their home and foreign mission work. Every church has the freedom to participate in any or all of the life and program of any unit of organization with which it is affiliated. The only actual authority of any organized unit is to accept or reject the church's affiliation. Most associations and conventions spell this out in their constitutions, while pointing out the right of the body to counsel with the churches where there seems to be the need.

Because of the free and autonomous nature of Baptist bodies, affiliation with them may be nearly as easily dissolved as it is established. No church is ever "bound" to the organization against its will. The associations and conventions are usually long-suffering and patient both with unhappy, indifferent, and unfaithful churches related to them. Churches are ordinarily patient also with the body of which they are a part. Rarely do denominational units exercise their option to remove churches from their fellowship. Rarely do churches request to be removed from affiliation.

In addition to the more formal relationships in associations and conventions, churches often relate to non-Baptist groups. In some cases they may formally relate to local organizations and movements in which they are interested. On a denominational level, this is always done in the framework of policies and procedures approved by the churches through their messengers at formal meetings and set out in constitutions, policy statements, or procedural outlines. On a local church level, this is at the discretion of that church. Various churches, motivated by their own sense of mission, their philosophy of work, and their personal interest, are related to other churches or other church groups as they choose.

Some churches relate to other churches in conferences or meetings of various sorts. They may sometimes share in projects in which they are interested. They may meet with others whenever they wish, formally or informally for whatever reason desired.

The Values of Affiliation

A legitimate and practical question that may be asked by any church considering affiliation with an association or convention or any other organization is, Of what value is this relationship to this church in its pursuit of its interpreted purpose in the mission of Christ? There are several practical values that may come to a church through affiliation with other churches in associations and conventions.

One of these is the development of confidence. Churches having good working relationships with other churches engender confidence. Attitudes make all the difference in the world as to what a church is and what it may accomplish in the world. While the confidence of a church in itself will rest foremost in its Lord, churches will find added confidence in good and wholesome relationships with other churches. Churches like people need peer support. A lack of trust is devastating to healthy church relationships. Being part of a true fellowship can do the same thing for churches that being a part of a good congregation can do for a Christian. When one feels he is not alone in what he is doing, he is encouraged and inspired. He is not overwhelmed by the task or fears that he will fail in his efforts. He knows there are others with him in his pilgrimage. They have the same basic beliefs and similar goals. Through good relationships, churches are encouraged by each other and develop greater confidence in themselves. They may dare to do more because they know they are not alone in what they are doing.

A second practical value is the maximum utilization of resources. Churches are usually able to employ more of their resources in a better way through cooperation with other churches than they can do alone. Every church has many resources within its membership, personal and otherwise. It never seems possible for a church to utilize all of the resources of its people with an isolated program. Out of a sense of stewardship of God-given life, talents, and abilities, which its members possess, a church wants to help its members "give themselves away" through the cooperative efforts of an organized program that reaches beyond themselves and calls them to their best efforts.

They may not be able to do this in a program confined just to their own membership. Through association and convention programs they have organized channels through which this may be done more effectively.

Perhaps one of the greatest values of church affiliation is ultimate accomplishment. Churches will ordinarily accomplish more working together with other churches than they can do alone. This is true whether through formal or informal participation. One of the greatest examples of this is what all kinds and sizes of Baptist churches have done in the support of mission work through the Cooperative Program, Southern Baptists' mission support program. The same may be said of what they have done through other programs such as associations where another type of cooperative effort is carried on. Churches broaden the scope of their ministries through their association and convention programs.

Maintaining Relationships

For churches to maintain good relationships, several things are necessary.

For one thing, everyone involved needs to have a good understanding of what their relationship with each other means. Proper concepts are crucial. For instance, to speak of the denomination or associations and conventions, some are likely to think in terms of the offices of the organization. Some may see the denomination as the people who work for the denomination, such as the director of missions, the executive directors, the consultants, and other officers or employees. In some ways it may be rightly said that there is really no such thing as "the denomination." The churches themselves are responsible for everything that goes on in their denomination or organization. The people who serve as officers are from the churches. The convention or association employees' salaries are paid from the churches. Members from the churches even wrote the charters and constitutions that govern all actions by association, conventions, boards, commissions, and committees. While officers, boards, and committees function freely, it is because of delegated authority given them by churches. The work of the association and convention is the churches working through their boards, agencies, and committees.

Therefore when the Baptist Press announces that the Foreign Mission Board has appointed missionaries, in reality it means that the churches have appointed missionaries through their Foreign Mission Board. The same could be said for the Home Mission Board. The churches affiliated through the Southern Baptist Convention print their own literature through their own Sunday School Board. They train their own preachers through their colleges and seminaries. They care for their retired preachers through their Annuity Board. The same thing can be said of every unit of organized Baptist life.

With this being true, churches have the responsibility of active participation in the affairs of their denomination. No church has a right to affiliate itself with other churches in a formal relationship without assuming its proportionate share of responsibility for that organization. This includes attending to business affairs through established procedures, sharing its resources in programs and services, and participating in its financial needs. It is never accurate for a Baptist to speak of the denomination as "they," but it is accurate to say "we" and "us" and "our." For an association or convention official to refer to the churches as "our churches" or to the pastors as "our pastors" may imply a denominational possession that is not intended or accurate. Churches are not possessed by denominations. Denominations belong to churches collectively affiliated.

Such a concept of the denomination lifts it from a distant and dull relationship, that may be passive in nature, to a personal, dynamic, and exciting way of getting the Lord's work done. The maintenance of such a concept requires constant attention by church leaders and denominational leaders alike.

The criteria for creating and maintaining a dynamic and meaningful relationship among churches may very well rest in three principles. For one thing, there will be individual church self-determination under Christ without intimidation or domination by others. Secondly, and conversely, there will be happy and wholesome church participation and cooperation without careless, unwarranted, or destructive condemnation of others. Thirdly, there will be full achievement and complete realization without self-glorification. If the relationships of a church are to be worthwhile, they must be good. Poor relationships may be worse than no relationships at all.

Value judgments are crucial for maintaining good relationships. The determination of what is important and what is not is vital to churches affiliated in associations and conventions. While the final determination of values rests with the churches, denominational leaders have a profound degree of responsibility to study needs, determine directions, and make plans for worthwhile cooperative efforts by Baptists. Both denominational leaders and individual church leaders often have to weigh many factors to determine the course they will plan and follow. Spiritual insights of Christian leaders often become blurred by personal interests, people pressures, and past successes. What God wants done is the ultimate desire of every Christian. To satisfy him requires subordination of strong wills, coordination of vast programs, and dedication to highest values by denominational leaders and churches. To pursue the plan of God is the most crucial factor faced by churches in any sort of relationship.

The enabling system of Southern Baptists may be unsurpassed in today's world and in Christian history. Through the highest and best use of all their relationships in all their units of organization, and through their commitment to the Scriptures and to the will of God, Baptists can find the right course, and through their organization, they have ways and means to do what they determine God wants them to do.

While there are many things to be realized from good relationships in Christian groups, perhaps the greatest satisfaction may not be in receiving but in giving. President John F. Kennedy expressed it profoundly when he was inaugurated. "Ask not what your country can do for you," he said, "ask what you can do for your country." So did Jesus express it, according to Luke's understanding in Acts 20:35 when he said, "It is more blessed to give than to receive." That is the spirit of relational Christianity.

8
The Growth of Churches
Quentin Lockwood

Should churches expect to grow? What are the areas in which a church should grow? How do churches grow? Should they plan to do so? What are the elements or factors found in a growing church? What keeps a church from growing? How can a church reverse itself if it is not experiencing growth?

Quentin Lockwood is an associate director in the Church Extension Department of the Home Mission Board of the Southern Baptist Convention. A native of Kentucky, he was graduated with the Associate of Arts degree in 1942, from Ashland Junior College, with the Bachelor of Arts degree in 1947, from Georgetown College, and the Bachelor of Divinity degree in 1950, from the Southern Baptist Theological Seminary.

Prior to coming to his present position in 1971, he had served as pastor of churches in Kentucky and Georgia as well as director of missions.

In the earlier chapters the kingdom of God and the churches' relationship to it has been discussed. The churches are not the kingdom of God but are part of the kingdom because their members are in the kingdom. Much of Jesus' teachings about the kingdom, particularly those related to the growth of the kingdom, can be applied to the churches. The principles of growth for the kingdom are the principles of growth for the churches.

Jesus taught that the kingdom of God would grow. The parables of the mustard seed, Matthew 13:31-32, the seed growing of itself, Mark 4:26-29, and leaven, Matthew 13:33, teach that the kingdom would grow, that it has the power within itself to grow and reproduce itself. It can be assumed that churches have in themselves the potency to grow and will grow. The teachings of Jesus give the foundations for growth. Acts and Paul's letters are the early record of growth, and church history is the continuing record of churches growing in the world, fulfilling Jesus' command to go into all the world (Matt. 28:19-20).

This growth can take several directions. It may be an inward growth as the members become more aware of what their commitment to Christ means. This results in a maturing of the believer and an increased Christlikeness in his life with an increase in fruitfulness. It may be an upward growth as the church worships and becomes more aware of God's presence and purpose for them. The church becomes more of a colony of God's people here on earth. Another direction of growth is outward. The first two should result in the last. The quality and depth of life resulting from inward and upward growth should cause the church to grow. The example of Christlikeness and the proclamation of the message of the kingdom will cause new people to be attracted to the kingdom so that a church will increase and new churches will be brought into existence.

A church should anticipate growth. A growing church should be the norm and not the exception. The parables of growth emphasize that the power to grow is inherent. Growth should be no surprise but a normal expression of the nature of the church. There should be the expectation of growth, and the churches should plan to accomplish this.

On the day of Jesus' ascension he gave his followers orders to be witnesses in Jerusalem, Judea, Samaria, and to the remote parts of the earth (Acts 1:8). As the people stood there awe struck, an angel said, "Why do you stand looking into the sky?" (Acts 1:11). Was he implying that they should get busy about this matter of Jerusalem, Judea, Samaria, and the remote parts of the world? Was he saying to them, "Get busy and start growing"?

The church in Jerusalem may not have understood all the implications of the Great Commission or going to the remote parts of the world, but as God's plan unfolded they accepted it, sometimes reluctantly. First there was the great congregation (or was it congregations?) in Jerusalem, then the scattering abroad preaching the word (Acts 8:4), some ending up in Phoenica, Cyprus, and Antioch (Acts 11:19). The churches were growing as the Word was proclaimed wherever persecution had scattered them.

Growth took its next step as the Holy Spirit spoke to the Antioch church and asked them to set Paul and Barnabas aside for "the work to which I have called them" (Acts 13:2). A new element entered the picture of churches growing. The Holy Spirit directed the church to send Paul and Barnabas to carry out a mission. For the first time a deliberate, planned effort was made to spread the gospel to areas that had not received it. Previous growth had been due to the scattering of the people because of persecution. The Holy Spirit was now revealing God's plan to reach the remote parts of the world as Paul and Barnabas set forth to spread the gospel, resulting in the planting of churches as converts were made. Two principles are revealed. The first is that church planting is God's work, and the second is that there is a plan. These two principles should not be ignored but should be incorporated into any plan for growing churches.

Three times a new work was attempted in Fremont. Once it progressed to the point of having a Sunday School, the other times it was a home fellowship. After the third attempt failed, no one went to Fremont for over two years. The missionary driving late one Sunday night across the prairie was seeking God's leadership about the next week's work. Fremont came to his mind. "I will go to Fremont and pick up my contacts next week," he said to himself. Tuesday afternoon he met one of the local pastors who said, "Guess what? I had two couples from Fremont in my church Sunday." Contact was made with these families and on Thursday night the missionary and the pastor met with three couples. That was the beginning of a new church in Fremont. It was God's time and plan for the new church.

The first principle could easily be distorted by saying it is God's work and only he can direct and lead in it. This is to ignore the second principle that shows church growth is part of a plan that requires the participation of the church. The church was to seek out, set aside, and send out Paul and Barnabas to do this work. Dr. W. O. Carver would say in his mission classes, "God's plan is a man," referring not only to what Christ did but also to the use of God's people in carrying out "God's plan for the ages." The church becomes a seeking out and sending agency as part of God's revealed plan.

The emerging pattern of a church may determine its attitudes toward growth and expansion. It took persecution to get the church out of Jerusalem, but after that the church took upon itself the matter of growth. Antioch sent out Paul and Barnabas. Someone took the gospel to Caesar's household (Phil. 4:22). Paul sought to go to Spain.

Everywhere the people went they shared Christ and churches were established. It was a deliberate effort to make Christ known. It was rooted in the fiber and being of these churches that Christ must be made known to everyone and churches established. Always it was in the framework of God's teaching. There was the Macedonian cry that turned Paul west rather than north. Were Paul's hinderances in going to Rome and on to Spain part of God's plan? Though not always explicitly stated, a reading of the story of the spread of the churches in the book of Acts reveals a sense of leadership beyond themselves. God's plan was being unrolled before them.

So it is today. Growth of the churches must conform to the two principles of growth. It is God's work and it should be planned. It can be said another way: Do something for God on purpose. In our day these principles should be instilled in each new church that comes into being and needs to be taught to the older churches that have forgotten or ignored them.

The early days of a newborn child often set the pattern for growth and actions for all the years ahead. The same is true of new churches. The early development is very important. Stunted growth and lack of outreach can result from a poor beginning. There are many factors that must be considered in a proper beginning of a church that will result in continuing growth.

A study of the New Testament pattern of church growth reveals several common factors in most of the new churches. There was first the proclamation or the preaching of the word (Acts 4:31; 12:24; 8:14; 13:44). The first message is the important one. They preached the word, God's word, the Christ. Peter's message to Cornelius (Acts 10:38-43) gives a good summary of the message preached. There was confirmation of God's anointing Jesus of Nazareth, his good life and deeds, his death on the cross, his resurrection on the third day, and the commission to preach to the people that in Jesus one's sins are forgiven. This central message lays the groundwork for all that is to follow in the church. A false or incomplete message here can doom the emerging congregation to a stunted, unfruitful growth.

As we follow Paul along his journeys, establishing new churches, we see another factor emerge. He enlisted leadership from those converted. There were few, if any, transplants from Jerusalem or Antioch. He had to staff that new church from the raw material at hand.

It was indigenous from the beginning! The people lived there, worked there, traded there; they were the community. Indigenous leadership is very important. Churches grow best when the leadership is part of the communities where the churches are located. The message is more acceptable from friends and peers than it is from strangers. In any new congregation the transition to indigenous leadership should be made as rapidly as possible. God's Spirit will lead in the searching out of those whom he wants to be the leaders.

In a large Midwestern city two churches were started on the growing edge of the city at about the same time. The communities were both new, about the same in size, one being slightly more affluent than the other. One immediately started growing in temporary quarters, the other grew more slowly, giving much time and attention to property and construction of a temporary facility. The first met in the schoolhouse and experienced rapid growth. Today one has more than seven hundred members, baptizes about fifty people per year, while the other has less than one hundred members and baptizes less than ten people per year. One has outgrown its facilities, the result of two building programs, and the other has yet to fill its first temporary unit. What caused the difference in the growth of the two? Several reasons can be advanced. The growing church has had only one pastor who preached a Christ-centered message with an emphasis on personal evangelism. It also placed emphasis on growing from the very beginning and quickly moved to indigenous leadership with a focus on people and not on facilities. The other had several short-term pastors, spent much time on getting facilities, and its leadership continued to be transplanted members from other areas. Today this church is dead, its property for sale.

Paul did not leave the leaders to their own devices. He spent time with them in teaching and training. This is yet another factor. Churches that grow have trained leadership. Acts 14:21-25 tells how Paul preached the gospel, strengthened the souls of the disciples, appointed elders in every church, and prayed with them before he returned to Antioch. In Antioch he stayed teaching and preaching (Acts 15:35) until the urge to "visit the brethren in every city in which we proclaimed the word of the Lord and see how they are" (Acts 15:36) had to be fulfilled. He traveled through Syria and Cilicia strengthening the churches (Acts 15:41). He also began to single out special ones to teach and train, such as Mark and Timothy. Not only did he see the need for training leaders in the churches but also to train leaders for the churches. His letters to the churches grew out of his continuing concern for helping them. He taught, he reprimanded, he praised, he condemned, always seeking to help these churches to be stable, growing communities. He sent Timothy to the Corinthian church to teach and to remind them of the things that he (Paul) had taught them (1 Cor. 4:17). Out of his letters comes the discovery that the churches cared for one another, even though they were diverse in language, culture, geography, and style. They took an offering for the poor in Jerusalem, they supported him in prison, and they commended members one to another. They were interrelated and caring because they were growing churches and there was a flow of members from one to the other.

Too much emphasis cannot be given to teaching and training the leaders of the churches. Teaching the correct things in the beginning days of the church will result in the right kind of leadership and proper growth. Ignorance of the things of God does not contribute to the growth of the churches.

There is not much insight into the kind of leadership that Paul enlisted in the new churches. The spread of the gospel and the growth of the churches indicate that they were leaders of ability and quality. The Jerusalem church chose men to lead who were "of good reputation, full of the Spirit and of wisdom" (Acts 6:3). First Timothy 3:1-13 gives the qualifications for those who seek the office of overseer and deacon, a high standard for leadership. This was the standard that was used in the selection of leaders. The best leaders possible should be chosen, taking into consideration the potential that each has to develop and grow. Much consideration should be given to those filled with the Spirit because the growing of churches is a spiritual endeavor. Good leadership has much to do with how well and how far the church grows.

The new church needs to prayerfully seek out those whom God would have to lead and begin to train them and teach them. Leadership must be sought out and developed. Too many did nothing because no one gave them work to do. Others have failed because no one trained them to do the task they were asked to perform. Paul sent Timothy to Thessalonica to strengthen (train) the leaders and encourage them in their faith (1 Thess. 3:2).

Much thought is often given to the physical location of a church. What did Paul do? We find him going to the strategic cities, to those where God led, to the central parts of those cities where the people were. It was in the synagogue, the marketplace, the stadium, the places where people congregated that he first preached the word. The essential ingredient for a church is people. People are the raw material from which churches are grown. The factor of going where the people are is still a valid one and should guide us in the planting of new churches. The church should never need to be sought out or hunted for, it should always be where the people are. It should not be like one of our pioneer churches located on four dead-end streets, backed up against two cemeteries, and accessible only by coming up a steep hill in an area of severe snow and ice conditions. Neither should it be like another, sitting in an orchard, midway between two small towns. It identified with neither and reached neither. How often we find the church meeting place in one location and the people in another. We preach to the scattered few rather than the gathered many.

Location is important. Perhaps not the exact corner or lot, but being where there are people is important. Some locations are more strategic than others. From some places growth of a church and growth through planting other churches can be more easily achieved than from others. Paul chose wisely where he should go and so should we.

The New Testament gives no record of anyone building a church house. They met where they could; on the Temple porch, in the synagogue, by the river, in a home, anywhere they could get some people together. They baptized in the pools, the rivers, and the seas. They took up offerings, they observed the Lord's Supper, they taught, they trained, and they planted new churches. They were concerned with building the kingdom of God and not with buildings. Their emphases were rightly placed. A new church meeting from place to place like the YMCA (they claimed the world's largest baptistry—the swimming pool); then a rented building; next a temporary church house; started five new churches in five years before they had a facility of their own and did all the things that a church should do.

Few churches today follow this pattern. We are church house oriented and sometimes locked into our church houses. The need for church houses was a natural outgrowth of the growth of the churches. Keep in mind the church came first and must always come first! First the church and then the building. This concept may be one answer to the cities of America. We could church the city by using public buildings, storefronts, temple porches, homes, street corners, and preaching the gospel without concern for buildings.

Buildings should be tools and not ends in themselves. Churches do not exist to build buildings but to build the kingdom and should only build what is needed to grow the church in that place. The facility may be either a promoter of growth or a hinderance to growth. If the facility becomes the center of interest in the church it becomes a detriment to growth. When a church says, "We have programmed around our building payment," concern for growth quickly dissipates. Churches do not exist to make building payments but to proclaim Christ. When a building is seen as a tool to be used, it can become a positive factor in growth. Churches contemplating building should seek the wisest counsel available before entering into design or construction.

Since all churches do not grow, consideration should be given to the causes of nongrowth. All causes of nongrowth are not easily identified, but some causes can be singled out.

The one that is most obvious is the lack of understanding of the missionary nature of the church. This has become so dim in the thinking of some churches that it has almost been lost completely. Akin to this is the false understanding that the missionary task is one that is done someplace else or that it can be hired done or that the giving of funds is what being missionary-minded is all about. This lack of understanding quickly brings a halt to the growth of the churches. When it is no longer seen as the responsibility of a church to grow or to extend itself, who is left to do it? There is no greater motivating factor in church growth than an understanding of the missionary nature of the church.

Another inhibiting factor to church growth is that of a continuous inward looking, where all actions are measured by what they do to enhance the group that now exists. What profits accrue to me?, is the cry. What will it cost? the compatriots echo. This self-centered approach denies the very nature of the church and leads it away from its fundamental task of growing. It makes the potent impotent.

In the come-to-me attitude of the church, we find another inhibitor of growth. The church reverses the role of the shepherd and the sheep. The shepherd now stays in the cote and the sheep must seek him rather than the shepherd seeking them. In God's dealing with man, he seeks man rather than man seeking him. The churches cannot play hide and seek with the lost world, asking people to find the church if they can. It is the church's role to aggressively seek those who are in need. Looking for the lost sheep is a primary task of the church.

Closely related to this is the danger of localizing the gospel, confining it to a certain place, to a building, even to a pulpit. Growing churches are ones that challenge the world with the gospel. It is taken into the streets and to the marketplace in an aggressive manner. The message of Christ must not become the captive of middle-class America but be brought to all people. How tragic it is that those who would profit most from the gospel are the last to hear!

Sometimes in our rush to build buildings, we create a hinderance rather than a help to growth. Certain styles of architecture often tend to keep people away. A high tier of steps leading to a massive door may be saying to some, If you can scale my steps and have the strength to pull open my doors, you may come into my darkness! This does not lend itself to growth. What an irony it is that many of our most ornate, massive, and expensive buildings sit in the midst of some of the most abject poverty and human need. We equate solemnity and low lights with God's presence when the Bible speaks of him as joy and light. Our overindulgence in buildings has led to unusual debts that consume a large percentage of church budgets, leaving little for the missionary cause of the church.

At times the facility may even become the object or focus of a type of worship. Proudly we note the stained-glass windows, while some have no windows. We point to the many-piped organ, while many hear no music, only the sound of a clamoring world. We point out our many rooms, while masses sleep in the streets or crowded in wretched hovels. This pride in our possessions is a far cry from the words of Peter and John to the lame man at the gate of the Temple. (Acts 3:6)

I sat one day in a building and watched the sun coming through a broken place in one of the stained-glass windows. As motes of dust danced in the sunlight, I began to wonder why anyone would throw a rock through such a lovely window. I recalled the community I had passed through to get to the church house and wondered if the rock were a challenge from someone saying, "Come out and see where I am." Was it someone saying, "What right do you have to a stained-glass window when I have no window at all?" Was it a cry of a burdened person, "Notice me—help me—please know that I am here?" Maybe the world was throwing down the gauntlet to the church, challenging them to come out of the sanctuary and translate worship into action.

The lack of vision can hinder the growth of the churches. When the lostness of the many around us is no longer a concern, there will be no growth. As the vision of the lostness of man diminishes so does the urgency to go to him with the gospel. When our hearts no longer cry out for the lostness of men and we cannot say with Paul that we would be willing to be accursed for our brethren, there will be a cessation of growth (Rom. 9:1-3; 10:1).

There are some remedial steps that a stunted church can take to start growing. They are not simple or easy. The first is that of self-examination. An honest self-evaluation is not easy but can be very productive. The letters to the seven churches in Asia, as recorded in Revelation, are a critique of each of them and calls on them to look at themselves. Ephesus is commended for its purity but condemned for its lost love. Smyrna is faithful in persecution, but Pergamus is chastised for tolerating evildoers. Thyatira is praised for her good deeds and scolded for tolerating Jezebel. Sardis is more dead than alive but has a few faithful left. Philadelphia has a door open for them, but lukewarm Laodicea is about to be spewed out. Each is admonished to look at themselves, to do some self-examination so that the weak will be strengthened and the strong will grow stronger. From these churches we can see that self-examination often calls for drastic and dramatic changes, but it is the first step to recovery of growth.

The Jerusalem church measured its growth as the numbers of converts are recorded (Acts 2:41; 2:47; 4:4; 6:7). It is wise to look at the numbers, to measure the growth or lack of growth. An audit of the books may reveal that not all is well in Churchville. A study of the church records can show whether growth is biological or extension growth. The church may just be reaching its own and not reaching the great number of the lost around them. Remedial measures can be considered when an accurate picture of growth is drawn.

The churches need to evaluate their programs, as well as their progress. Things that are working right should be commended and efforts made to further improve them. Nonfunctioning or poorly functioning programs should be carefully evaluated to see what is wrong and how they can be made to work effectively. Gaps in programming should be looked for and plugged.

Some questions that should be asked are, Where do we touch the lost world? Where is our major emphasis? Where does our church budget and staff place its emphasis?

The biggest question of all is, Does the church really want to grow? There will be no growth until the church decides it must grow and that it wants to grow. Answering the question about a church recovering its real nature and embarking on a course of planned church growth is not easily answered or lightly taken. Recovery of the true missionary nature of the church can be a slow process, often like that of a patient recovering from an illness. The medicine may taste bad, the cost may be high, the cure long in coming, pain may be experienced, but the end results are worth it.

9

The Holy Spirit and the Birth of Churches

J. Terry Young

Has some dimension of the Holy Spirit's work been overlooked or neglected today? Who is the Holy Spirit? What is his relationship to the church? How was the Holy Spirit related to churches in the book of Acts? What part did he play in the unfolding of the history of churches in Scripture? What is the function of the Holy Spirit in churches today? Is he interested in the beginning of new churches? What does he do in the area of church planting?

J. Terry Young is professor of theology at the New Orleans Baptist Theological Seminary. A native of Texas, he was graduated with the Bachelor of Arts degree in 1951, from Baylor University, then with the Bachelor of Divinity degree in 1955, and the Doctor of Theology degree in 1962, from Southwestern Baptist Theological Seminary.

He has served as pastor of churches in Texas and California and as editor of the California Southern Baptist. *He has written numerous articles for various Baptist periodicals and other publications. He is also the author of two books published by Broadman Press:* The Spirit Within You *(1977) and* The Church Alive and Growing *(1978).*

New churches are born periodically because the Holy Spirit of God is still at work in God's world. Indeed, apart from the work of the Holy Spirit there would be no new churches or any old churches either. The Holy Spirit is the life of the church; he is the One who gives life and vitality to the church. He is the presence of the living Christ. He is the heartbeat of the church which the New Testament describes as the body of Christ. The Holy Spirit is the source of the growth of the church, both intensively and extensively. Intensively, the Spirit leads a church in its process of spiritual growth, the process of maturing in character, and usefulness in the service of God. Extensively, he is responsible for the church duplicating itself in the birth of new church congregations, as well as winning new converts to Christ.

Who is this Holy Spirit who is so deeply involved in the birth and life of churches? On the one hand, some people have virtually overlooked his indispensable role in the life of the church. On the other hand, some have distorted his role. Perhaps there are even more people who have simply taken the work of the Holy Spirit for granted as they have gone about the work of the church.

Most people who have been involved in planting new churches are keenly aware of the essential work of the Holy Spirit in the birth and life of churches. No more dramatic evidence of the relationship of the Holy Spirit to the extension of the church can be seen than in the work of the Holy Spirit in the first steps of the church on the day of Pentecost (Acts 1—2). This was the day that the church was energized with the divine presence and empowered for its mission of being witness to Jesus unto the uttermost parts of the earth.

Some say that the day of Pentecost marked the birth of the church. That is probably putting it a little too strongly. The church, as a group of people called out under the lordship of Jesus Christ, ought to be traced back at least to the great confession of Peter at Caesarea-Philippi. At Caesarea-Philippi Jesus asked his twelve disciples who the crowds were saying that he was. They gave varying answers. Then he asked them who they thought he was. Peter answered for the group, "Thou art the Christ, the Son of the living God" (Matt. 16:16). Jesus responded, "Upon this rock I will build my church; and the gates of Hades shall not overpower it" (Matt. 16:18). In reality, then, the Christian church had its beginning here, but it waited until the day of Pentecost to take its first steps in penetrating the world with its message of the gospel of the Lord Jesus Christ.

In Jesus' last command to his disciples, according to Luke's Gospel, Jesus told his followers to wait in Jerusalem until the Holy Spirit should come upon them (Luke 24:49). The presence of the Holy Spirit was essential for the church to begin fulfilling its God-appointed ministry of being witness to Jesus, penetrating the world with the gospel of new life. While there was a church before Pentecost, it was, in a sense, an incomplete church. It needed the presence and work of the Holy Spirit within it to be able to function as the body of Christ. It was in a position of waiting to take its first steps as a church. Prior to the coming of the Spirit on the day of Pentecost, the church was not ready to begin its ministry of spreading the gospel. The movement of the Spirit upon the church on the day of Pentecost was the inauguration of the church in its missionary movement.

When the Holy Spirit came upon the church on the day of Pentecost, things began to happen (Acts 2:37-47). The church was transformed and the period of waiting was over! The members of the church had a vivid new consciousness of who they were as a church, and they had a strong sense of motivation to begin spreading the good news of the gospel. This is not to say that they did not have a missionary motivation before the Spirit came upon them, neither is it to say that they did not have a self-consciousness of being the church, the body of Christ. It is to say, however, that there was a tentativeness, an incompleteness about the church, prior to the coming of the Spirit on the day of Pentecost. When the Spirit came upon the church, a profound transformation took place: The church now became a people on mission for their Lord.

The mission of the church inaugurated by the coming of the Holy Spirit was manifested in several ways. Immediately there was a dramatic revival on the day of Pentecost. Three thousand converts were swept into the fellowship of the church in one day (Acts 2:41). The church began to evidence spiritual growth and dedication, at least among some of its people, even in the face of severe problems and hardships (Acts 2:44-47a). The numerical growth of the church was rather startling (Acts 2:47b).

At first there apparently was no idea of there being anything other than one central congregation serving all Christians, just as there had been only one Temple serving all Judaism. But it was not long until the church began planting new congregations all over the Mediterranean world. And this business of planting new congregations, new churches, was a direct result of the work of the Holy Spirit in the church. But that story shall be unfolded a little later. First, let us ask a serious question at this point which will help us to understand better the work of the Holy Spirit in the church in its ever-widening circles of planting Christian churches in unreached territory.

Who is the Holy Spirit? Precisely what is his role, according to the New Testament? [1] It ought not to be necessary to ask such questions, but there is such widespread misunderstanding concerning the

Holy Spirit today that it is wise to focus momentarily on who the
Holy Spirit is and what he does. Our Christian belief focuses upon
one God who makes himself known to us in three persons. We have
traditionally called these three persons the Trinity, though the term
itself is not a biblical one. For a correct understanding you must
focus upon both the one and the three at the same time. The three
persons of the Trinity must not be seen as separate, distinct persons,
standing independently of each other. That would be tritheism rather
than trinitarianism, three gods rather than one. Neither must the
distinctions be swallowed up in giving exclusive attention to the unity.
The three distinctions of Father, Son, and Holy Spirit are real distinctions, but the three also share a common life, an identity. Virtually
anything that is said of one person of the Trinity must be said about
the other two also.

No rigid distinctions must be drawn between God the Father, God
the Son, and God the Holy Spirit. What is true of one is also true
of the other two. What one does, the other two are involved in also.
The Holy Spirit has been intimately involved in the work of God
the Father from the very beginning. In fact, Genesis 1:1-2 shows
that the Spirit was involved in the work of creation. His work can
be seen at numerous points in the Old Testament. The day of Pentecost is by no means the beginning of his work in the world.

In the same way, Christ was also involved with the Father in creation.
John 1:3 indicates that Christ was the agent of creation, that nothing
was made that was not made through him, a thought repeated in
Colossians 1:16. The Bible says then that God created the heavens
and the earth, that Jesus was the Creator, and that the Holy Spirit
was also involved in creation. Other examples could be cited to show
that the work of one of the three persons of the Trinity is also the
work of the other two persons.

In the New Testament, the relationship is so close that there is
almost an identity between Jesus and the Holy Spirit (2 Cor. 3:17).
As Jesus was preparing his disciples for his departure from them,
he promised that he would not leave them alone. In John 14:16 he
promised them *another* Comforter, or Helper, to take his place. The
word *another* in this instance is one which has the force of another
of the same kind—one who will be just like Jesus, one who will be
to them just what he has been. In John 14:18, Jesus said to his sorrow-

ing disciples that he himself would come unto them, a verse which cannot have been a reference to his second coming. He was evidently viewing the coming of the Holy Spirit as his own coming to them. The coming of the Holy Spirit was not the introduction of some third divine being to take the place of Jesus. As Jesus had previously taught his disciples that he and the Father are one, so he was now indicating that he and the Holy Spirit are virtually one. The point in all of this is that the work of the Holy Spirit in the church *is* the work of Jesus Christ, who is the head of the church. The work of Jesus in the church, in turn, is the work of God the Father in the church.

The Holy Spirit is, then, the presence of Jesus in his church, dwelling in the hearts of the people who make up the church. As Jesus once had been physically present with his disciples in a particular place, he is now present universally—everywhere, at the same time—with all of his followers. The work of the Holy Spirit is none other than the same work that God has been doing from the beginning and brought to a climax in the life, death, and resurrection of Jesus Christ.

The Holy Spirit is the presence of God in the world bringing men to conviction, leading them through the new birth, developing them in Christian growth, and leading them in churches to extend the faith through the outreach of the churches and the planting of new churches in locales beyond the immediate vicinity of existing churches.

The book of Acts is an interesting study of the work of the Holy Spirit in the developing church. It is here seen that a primary function of the Holy Spirit in the church is to lead it in missionary expansion, reaching people and planting churches. In most of our Bible translations the book of Acts bears the title "The Acts of the Apostles." Actually, the title does not belong with the book, as none of the books of the Bible originally had titles. Many interpreters feel that the book of Acts would have been better named "The Acts of the Holy Spirit" since the Holy Spirit is the most prominent character in the book. It is his story that is unfolding as he is directing the church.

In an obvious reference to the Gospel which he had written earlier, Luke began Acts, saying, "The first account I composed, Theophilus, about all that Jesus began to do and teach" (Acts 1:1). The apparent implication is that this second book (Acts) is what Jesus *continued* to do and teach. Yet, the book centers upon the leadership of the Holy Spirit. Jesus figures into the book only as the subject preached by the church which is being directed by the Holy Spirit. Apparently, in Luke's mind there was little, if any, difference in what Jesus began and what the Holy Spirit continued to do in Acts.

But let's go back now to the story of the Holy Spirit and the first steps of the church in Jerusalem. The church had an instant revival with thousands swept into the church. But that was not all. The story is not all good. The church had to learn some difficult lessons before it was really ready to do the work that God had in mind for it to do.

The church in Jerusalem was at first afflicted with the same kind of nearsightedness that had afflicted Israel as the chosen servant-people of God throughout her whole history. The church had a hard time understanding that the gospel was for all men, in spite of the fact that the Great Commission had set the boundaries of the Christian mission at the uttermost parts of the earth (Matt. 28:19-20; Acts 1:8). At first, it seems to have seen itself as primarily Jewish, still attached to the Temple and the traditions of Judaism. Many of the Christians continued to worship in the Temple until the friction between Jews and Christians made that virtually impossible.

Even when the church cut the ties to Temple worship, the Christians had a difficult time understanding that Christianity was for all people. When Philip, one of the seven deacons chosen by the Jerusalem church, ranged far and wide preaching the gospel, some Samaritans were converted (Acts 8:4-13). Likely, many at Jerusalem were not ready to accept Samaritan converts. So, the church sent Peter and John to Samaria where they indeed found a response to the preaching of the gospel (Acts 8:14-17). While they were there Peter and John prayed for these believers and laid hands upon them, a sign of their blessing, and the Holy Spirit came upon these Samaritan converts just as he had on the Jerusalem church on the day of Pentecost. This was a strong demonstration to the Jerusalem church that God was thrusting his church truly into all of the world with a gospel that was intended for all people.

But the lesson still was not complete. It remained for the church, which still had strongly Jewish sentiments, to learn that "all the world" included Gentiles as well as Samaritans. The Holy Spirit again figured prominently into leading the church over this racial barrier. Cornelius, a God-fearing Gentile with certain sympathies for the Jews, was directed in a vision to send for Simon Peter (Acts 10:1-6). On the other end of the line, Peter himself had a remarkable vision, brought to him by the Holy Spirit, in which he was told that he should not call anything unclean that God has cleansed (Acts 10:9-16).

Somewhat reluctantly—it took Peter twice as long to get to Caesarea where Cornelius was as it had taken Cornelius' servant to come to Peter—Peter went to Cornelius. After Peter proclaimed the gospel to Cornelius, Cornelius responded in faith and was converted. Again, to drive home the point with Peter and with those back at home who would be reluctant to believe that the gospel was truly for Gentiles as well as Jews, the Holy Spirit came upon Cornelius and his household as on the day of Pentecost (Acts 10:34). God was blessing the preaching of the gospel to Gentiles in the same way as he was in the church back in Jerusalem.

Even after these remarkable demonstrations through the work of the Holy Spirit that the gospel is for *all* men, without restriction or qualification, the church still had not fully learned the lesson. Some preached the gospel only to Jews (Acts 11:19). And some of the members of the church wanted to impose the Jewish ceremonial requirements of circumcision and other ritual observances upon Gentile converts (Acts 15:1). It took a council of representatives of the church, meeting in Jerusalem, to decide once and for all that the Christian church is not just an extension of Judaism, that it is the body of Christ's followers who had a Jewish heritage but with a complete, separate identity of its own. When this Jerusalem Council announced its findings, notice how they phrased it. "For it seemed good to the Holy Spirit and to us" (Acts 15:28). The Holy Spirit was intimately involved in the growth and extension of the church, and that at some very significant points. The chief function of the Holy Spirit in the life of the church was to prod and lead it in extension.

It is not clear in the New Testament record when the church at Jerusalem and the church as found elsewhere began to take on separate identities as different congregations. For awhile it is fairly clear that the Christians, wherever they happened to be, were simply part of one church. Only gradually did the separate congregations come into an identity of their own. But it becomes evident after awhile

that the focus shifts from the church to the churches, local congregations of Christians in various places.

This multiplication of churches, in the outward spread of the gospel,
was itself the work of the Holy Spirit. It was no accident or coincidence
that the church was planted at Antioch. And the Antioch church came
to overshadow the Jerusalem church in importance.

The first formal missionary thrust of the church came from the
Antioch church. According to Acts 13:1-3, it was the action of the
Holy Spirit that sent the first two missionaries on the first missionary
journey. "And while they were ministering to the Lord and fasting,
the Holy Spirit said, 'Set apart for me Barnabas and Saul for the
work to which I have called them' " (Acts 13:2). The church responded
and sent them on their way. The result of this first missionary journey
by Paul, and of two later journeys, was the establishment of churches.
As you read the rest of the New Testament, you discover that there
were churches in cities scattered all over the Mediterranean world.

These missionary journeys which produced churches where Paul
and his companions labored had more than human direction. They
were under divine guidance. Just as the Holy Spirit had moved the
church to send forth the first two missionary preachers, so the Holy
Spirit guided them along the way and blessed their efforts.

There is a powerful illustration of the work of the Holy Spirit in
directing the missionary labors of Paul. According to Acts 16:6-10,
the Spirit of God was quite specific in his leading of Paul, forbidding
him to turn first one way and then another. Finally, Paul had a notable
vision during the night of a man of Macedonia saying, "Come over
to Macedonia and help us" (Acts 16:9).

The Holy Spirit was intimately involved in the rapid expansion of
early Christianity. The church had a small, inauspicious beginning
in Jerusalem under circumstances which, humanly speaking, would
have seemed enough to guarantee the failure of so bold an enterprise
as that of the church. Only divine direction could have brought the
little band of Jesus' followers to the success they enjoyed in planting
churches in cities all over the Mediterranean world, including Rome
itself. It seems to be a fair conclusion that one of the major works
of the Holy Spirit in the New Testament age was that of planting
new churches. If you follow the story on through history, you will

see that in every age the Holy Spirit has been bringing churches to birth.

There is no such thing as a free-lance Christianity, a Christianity apart from churches. Generally speaking, where you have converts being brought from death to life through the new birth, you also have churches being born. Many Christians, obviously, are associated with previously existing churches. But as the number of Christians grows, and as cities and communities grow, so the number of churches also grows.

The Holy Spirit is as concerned today with planting new churches as he was in the days of the first faltering steps of the church. Indeed, he is constantly trying to enlarge the vision of the churches to see the opportunities for planting new churches. The modern church, like the ancient church, tends all too often to have a narrower vision than does its Lord. Just as of old, it needs to be nudged and prodded. It needs occasionally to catch a Macedonian vision.

What is the role of the Holy Spirit in the life of the church today? In recent years so much has been written and said about the relationship of the Holy Spirit to the individual Christian life that many have tended to lose sight of the full work of the Spirit, especially in relation to the church. As some have focused almost exclusively upon speaking in tongues and other "charismatic gifts," they have lost the biblical perspective on the work of the Holy Spirit.

We cannot institutionalize the Holy Spirit or confine him to the church, but we must also remember that just as conversion and the Christian life are vitally related to the church in the New Testament, so the work of the Holy Spirit is intimately associated with the life of the church. Thus, any talk of planting churches must give careful attention to the subject of the role of the Spirit in bringing new churches to birth and maturity. The work of the Holy Spirit in the church is indispensable. Without him the church would have no life, certainly no vitality such as is needed to bring new churches to birth.

Several things should be said about the work of the Holy Spirit in the church. First and foremost, it should be noticed that the Holy Spirit is the effective agent in the church's proclamation of the gospel. It is not human expertise or persuasiveness that brings converts to Christ. It is the persuasive power of the Holy Spirit that produces conviction, repentance, and faith within the heart of a sinner. Jesus indicated in John 16:8-11 that this is the function of the Holy Spirit. The church needs to realize that it is dependent upon the action of the Holy Spirit to bring men to conversion. Whatever efforts a church puts forth only provide the occasion for the Holy Spirit to do his work.

In saying that it is the Holy Spirit who produces converts it should not be understood that the church has no part in the success of the proclamation of the gospel. The Holy Spirit chooses to work through the human efforts that we put forth, and the more vigorous and varied our efforts, the better the opportunity that the Holy Spirit has to do his work of producing a spiritual harvest. Our busyness does not guarantee the presence and work of the Holy Spirit. Our efforts only furnish him the opportunity to work. Properly understood, the church is absolutely dependent upon the work of the Spirit for any effectiveness in its efforts to reach men for Christ.

We must also remember that when men are converted, it is the work of the Holy Spirit that produces the spiritual change—the new birth—in them. The Holy Spirit is the effective agent of salvation. It is the coming of the Spirit of God into the life of an individual that makes of him a Christian. The coming of the Spirit into his life is the entrance of God himself into that person's life. This is what Jesus was saying in his interview with Nicodemus, as recorded in John 3, where Jesus told Nicodemus that he would have to be born again.

In addition, according to Ephesians 4:7-13, the Holy Spirit is at work in the church building up the church, equipping the church for its ministry. This passage, and similar passages in Romans 12 and 1 Corinthians 12, picture the Holy Spirit bestowing gifts of service upon the members of the church, welding them into a functioning body for Christ's service. In addition, the Holy Spirit leads the church members into Christian ministry, leading them to produce the fruits of the Spirit or Christlike qualities (Gal. 5:22-23).

The work of the Spirit of God is also to lead the church in the progress of its work. Even as the Holy Spirit gave quite specific guidance to Paul and his companions on their missionary journeys, so the Holy Spirit today offers guidance to the churches. The tragedy is that many do not avail themselves of the guidance that is open to them. We need to cultivate a sense of the presence and leadership of the Spirit of God in our churches. The same Jesus who said to his disciples, "Behold, I say to you, lift up your eyes, and look on the fields, that they are white for harvest" (John 4:35), is still trying to get his followers to see the opportunities at hand.

We claim that Jesus is the Head of the church, that he is the Lord of the church—and that he is. But that headship, that lordship, is exercised through the presence of the Holy Spirit in the church to give it guidance and spiritual power. The church is described as the body of Christ in the world. Some even describe the church as a continuing incarnation. Whether you accept the terminology or not, that designation indicates an important truth. The church is the chosen instrument of God for service in the world today. And the Holy Spirit is continually offering guidance to the church.

Surely one of the things that God is trying to do through his church today is to extend the reach of the good news of salvation through Jesus Christ, the good news of new life for a dying world. Part of that task falls in the category of evangelism through the local church. Part of it falls in the category of what we have traditionally called missions.

A vital part of what God is trying to get his churches to do today in a world with a mushrooming population, and the constant spread of urban sprawl in great metropolitan centers, is to plant new churches. While the church cannot ever cease its evangelistic labors in its own local setting, the church can best fulfill its responsibilities in evangelism by establishing new congregations, planting new churches in areas not immediately served by a good, evangelical church. This, in part, is what Jesus was saying when he indicated that the fields are white unto harvest. There is no lack of possibilities for reaching men with the gospel and growing them into churches right in their own communities.

It just may be that one of the primary things the Spirit of God is trying to do today is to get the churches to catch a vision of planting new churches. While we must always strive for the internal development of the churches that we already have, we must never make the mistake of thinking that the birth of new churches can wait for another day. There is a generation of people all about us now who need churches to minister to them—and there are not enough vital churches to serve their needs.

The focus comes down to this when we are talking about the Holy Spirit and the birth of churches. A vital function of the Holy Spirit in the continuing Christian task is in the realm of planting churches as part of a vigorous, planned attempt to take the gospel to the uttermost parts of the earth. One of the continuing problems in this matter is that the church today is beset with some of the same problems of ancient Judaism, and of the early church as well. We are beset with the problem of spending more time gazing inward upon ourselves than in gazing outward to fields that are white unto harvest. We are beset with a certain spiritual inertia or spiritual nearsightedness.

That precise problem is one of the reasons that the Holy Spirit came into the world. In terms of Joel's prophecy of the coming of the Holy Spirit, the function of the Holy Spirit is to break that spiritual inertia and nearsightedness. When Joel told of the coming of the Spirit, several hundred years before Pentecost, he stated it beautifully and dramatically.

"Your old men will dream dreams,
Your young men will see visions" (Joel 2:28, author's italics).

Vision is one of the key essentials in the planting of new churches today. We are dependent upon the Holy Spirit to give us a vision of the opportunities that are ours in bringing new churches to birth. Imparting this vision is but one of four tasks the Holy Spirit accomplishes in the church today with regard to planting new churches. But it is an essential task. The visions Joel was talking about were not some sort of ecstatic experiences. Perhaps the dreams and visions Joel saw as part of the work of the Holy Spirit were those holy ambitions God implants in the hearts of his people when he wants some noble task accomplished. Paul saw a vision of the man of Macedonia calling to him for help (Acts 16:9-10) and as a result the gospel was introduced to Europe, and today the Western world has been strongly influenced by Christianity.

This stirring of the Spirit of God, giving man a vision of an unmet need, is what led one young pastor to resign a comfortable church and move into a new residential community to seek to start a new church. There were no public buildings that could be utilized as a temporary meeting place for a church. So, the pastor simply started the church in the little home that he had purchased. In just a few weeks his home would not accommodate the people they were reaching. So, they rented a washateria that was not used on Sundays. There, amidst the washers and dryers, the little congregation grew. Finally, after nearly two years, the church was able to buy a piece of property on the edge of the developing community and with volunteer labor erect the first unit of several planned units for their church facilities. In not many years, the church was one of the leading churches in that whole area. And all because the Holy Spirit planted a vision in the heart of a young pastor and then a few other faithful Christians.

This simple story could be repeated in numerous similar illustrations of how the Holy Spirit plants a vision in the heart of a congregation, urging it to bring a new church to birth in an area that is not adequately churched. Sometimes the vision is implanted in the hearts of just a few people and later spreads to others. God is seeking to nudge his church into ever-widening circles through the planting of new churches.

A second work of the Holy Spirit in the planting of new churches is providing the motivation necessary to accomplish the task (Acts 13:1-3). This work of motivation, performed by the Holy Spirit, is obviously not limited to the one matter of planting new churches. Many a church would be highly profited if it could realize that motivating the people of the church to any of their tasks in the life of the church is best performed by the Holy Spirit. Some churches which have long relied on promotional gimmicks and high-pressure tactics to produce motivation have proven to their own dismay that such motivation produced by human manipulation and pep-rally enthusiasm is superficial and difficult to maintain. Indeed, many of them have come to realize that the gimmicks and schemes inevitably run out and the church is left with a motivational crisis.

True and lasting motivation in the life of the church comes from the stirring of the Holy Spirit in the hearts of the people (Acts 4:32-37). One group of people were so motivated in beginning a new church that they gave their savings and mortgaged their homes in order to raise enough money to make the large down payment required to purchase a piece of property for their new congregation. No human promotional scheme could have led these average wage earners to make the kind of sacrifice they made to bring a new church to birth.

The same Spirit of God which produced this sacrificial motivation in the hearts of this group of people continued to guide and nurture this church. The church experienced substantial growth. In just a few years the church found that the piece of property they had thought would be large enough for many years was about to be too small. And to complicate the problem, they knew that the adjoining property was not for sale at any price.

The church again relied on the leadership of the Holy Spirit. They spent a great deal of time in prayer about the matter. In fact, they called a special week of prayer services to give earnest prayer to the future of their church. Before the week was over, the owners of the property next to the church, not knowing what had been going on during the week, approached the church with an offer to sell their property to the church at a reasonable price.

With that kind of answer to prayer, the church was again motivated to raise from its seemingly limited resources a rather substantial sum of money to make it possible to buy the property which was now available to them. Through all of this the Holy Spirit was the guiding, motivating force that brought this church into existence and then led it through numerous critical steps. And the people of the church were very much aware that the success that they had enjoyed was due to the work of the Holy Spirit, blessing their efforts and guiding them each step of the way.

In the third place the Holy Spirit provides the resources for planting new churches and guiding them to maturity (Eph. 4:11-16; 1 Cor. 12:1-31). There are many things needed in the planting of new churches. Vision and motivation are not all. Once the conviction and determination are clear that there should be a new church brought into being, there are still many things that new church will need. The Holy Spirit is the best possible resource for all of the needs that a church, new or old, might ever have (2 Cor. 12:9; Eph. 4:19).

There are needs for leadership. A new congregation must have a pastor, Sunday School teachers, and a variety of other workers to carry out the various tasks of winning and developing people as Christians. It was noted earlier that one of the functions of the Holy Spirit in the life of the church, according to Ephesians 4 and similar passages, is equipping the members of the church with gifts of service. The Holy Spirit often lays a burden upon the heart of some church member and implants within him a desire to render some particular kind of service in the life of the church. The same Spirit of God leads him to develop the know-how, the ability to perform the particular task in question.

The Holy Spirit also furnishes to the church the wisdom and divine guidance that a church must have if it is to be successful in its work. Jesus made many promises to the church concerning the effectiveness of prayer. James 1:5 indicates that if one lacks wisdom, he may ask God for it and receive it freely given. As Jesus promised in the Great Commission, the church does not stand alone in its work of penetrating the world with the gospel. It always has the presence of the Lord within (Matt. 28:19-20). And that presence is not merely to lend companionship or comfort. It is to lend support and guidance.

A fourth provision of the Holy Spirit for the church in the birth of new churches is the blessing of a harvest. As it is promised in Scripture that the preaching of the word of God will not be in vain, so the Holy Spirit blesses the church with a harvest, with effectiveness in its work. We who serve in the church are not limited to what our own efforts and expertise can accomplish. We have the assurance that the Spirit of God will utilize our efforts and bless them with a degree of effectiveness (1 Cor. 3:5-8; Isa. 55:10-11; Matt. 13:31-32).

There really isn't as much reason for churches to be as hesitant to bring new churches to birth as they often are. The Holy Spirit of God is vitally concerned to bring new churches to birth and then to maturity. He has been from the day of Pentecost on, and he always will be. The chief problem is that in our preoccupation with the needs of our existing churches, we fail to perceive the Spirit's dimensions of work through new congregations. Sometimes that may be because of a self-centered interest. We are afraid that a new congregation might siphon off leadership and money that would have supported the mother church. Some churches have been pleasantly surprised that the leadership and financial support invested in creating a new church actually strengthened, rather than weakened, the mother church. The Holy Spirit blessed both churches with the necessary resources.

Perhaps we do not bring more churches to birth because of a lack of faith. We do not really believe that God can do in this age what he did in other ages (Jas. 4:2*b*; Matt. 17:20). But the Holy Spirit who brought about a mighty harvest of conversions on the day of Pentecost and dotted the Mediterranean world with churches can still do the same thing today. Indeed, he is doing it through some groups which are growing very rapidly both in total membership and in the number of congregations. The Holy Spirit is not hampered by a lack of power or a lack of resources for the business of planting new churches today. If he is limited at all, it is only by our own lack of faith, our lack of willingness to be used of him in the marvelous task of bringing a new church to life.

A spirit of institutionalism may impede the work of the Holy Spirit in bringing new churches to birth. Some churches get caught up in the spirit of bigness, building bigger facilities, hiring larger staffs, and conducting ever larger programs. There may not be anything wrong with this. But if all of this is being done at the expense of refusing to bring new congregations to birth in areas that need a ministering church in the immediate vicinity, then institutionalism has taken its sad toll.

Surely no one would want to say that God sets an arbitrary limit on the size a church ought to be allowed to reach. At the same time, however, let us remember that the larger a church becomes, the less efficient it is in reaching people with the gospel. There are some things that the large church can do better than the small, new church can. We need the large, strong churches. But the small, new church enjoys a ratio of converts to total membership that the large church cannot possibly reach.

This observation alone would impel us to say that the Spirit of God is vitally concerned today with the establishment of new churches. It simply is a proven fact that new churches will usually reach more people with the gospel than old, settled churches.

This present generation has devoted more attention to the subject of the Holy Spirit than has any previous generation. However, much of the attention given to the study of the Holy Spirit has been misleading. And in most of this misguided study, little attention has been given to the work of the Holy Spirit in evangelism and missions, particularly to his role in the planting of new churches. This may have been one of the key roles of the Holy Spirit in the New Testament age.

If we really want to be biblical in the emphasis being given to the Holy Spirit today, we ought to give more attention to the subject of his involvement in the birth of churches. Any genuine sensitivity to the leadership of the Holy Spirit in the church today ought to produce not only a host of new converts and a succession of people maturing in Christian faith and character but also a considerable increase in the numbers of churches being born.

Note

1. For a full discussion of the biblical doctrine of the Holy Spirit, see J. Terry Young, *The Spirit Within You* (Nashville: Broadman Press, 1977).